# EM MODO DE HAIKU

# IN HAIKU MODE

LEONOR CAPELLA

2023

Chapbook Press

Schuler Books
2660 28th Street SE
Grand Rapids, MI 49512
(616) 942-7330
www.schulerbooks.com

Em Modo de Haiku – In Haiku Mode

ISBN 13: 9781957169347

Library of Congress Control Number: 2023902397

**Printed in the United States by Chapbook Press.**

In Haiku Mode

Im Haiku-Modus

En Mode Häiku

En Modo de Haiku

## Agradecimentos

Gostaria de deixar aqui expresso o meu profundo agradecimento às pessoas que me ajudaram a realizar o sonho muito antigo de publicar um livro de haikus. Estou grata à minha irmã Dra. Teresa Castelão-Lawless, professora universitária nos Estados Estados Unidos da América, que participou ativamente nas várias versões dos textos e na pesquisa das fotos para a capa do livro. Relativamente ao trabalho editorial das várias línguas em que escrevi os meus haikus, quero agradecer à minha grande amiga Dra. Fátima Quitério, médica de Saúde Pública na Direção Geral de Saúde e que fez a revisão do espanhol, e à Ana do Deutsch-Lernstudio do Goethe Institut em Lisboa por ter contatado professores deste instituto para editarem o alemão. Finalmente, agradeço ao meu editor Pierre Camy, da Chapbook Press nos Estados Unidos da América, que corrigiu o francês e participou ativamente no processo de construção do meu livro com disponibilidade e profissionalismo.

## Acknowledgements

I would like to thank all those who helped me bring to life an old dream of publishing a book of haikus. I am grateful to my sister, Dr. Teresa Castelão-Lawless, a University professor in the United States of America, who participated actively in the various versions of the text as well as research on the photos for the book cover. As it pertains to the editorial work on the different languages in which I wrote my haikus, I would like to thank my great friend Dr. Fátima Quitério, public health physician at the Direção Geral de Saúde in Lisbon who edited the Spanish, and Ana of the Deutsch-Lernstudio of the Goethe Institut in Lisbon who contacted teachers there to correct the German. Finally, I want to express my gratitude to my editor Pierre Camy at Chapbook Press, who corrected the French and participated actively in the process of construction of my book with availability and professionalism.

## Introdução

Não recordo de como tive os primeiros contactos com a forma de poesia japonesa haiku, mas sei que imediatamente me interessou, porque achei muito bonito e poético, e, até, pelo menos aparentemente, simples, e logo me encantou porque o haiku é uma forma condensada, telegráfica, de expressão, muito de acordo com a minha maneira de ver e organizar o mundo. Uma poesia da natureza, tão diferente da verborreia, politização e sexualização na poesia ocidental. Não pretendo de modo algum desvalorizar a poesia da civilização em que nasci, há muito boa poesia ocidental, mas para mim a leveza dos haikus exerce um fascínio especial.

Não deixa de ser curioso que uma forma poética, criada há mais de 400 anos, para uma época, cultura, língua, e escrita tão diferente da(s) ocidental(ais) possa ter resultado numa transposição tão improvável. E, mais do que isso, permitir que pudessem ser criados nessas e outras línguas, mantendo muito do seu encanto original.

Ao longo do tempo fui adquirindo e lendo livros, tanto físicos como digitais, sobre o assunto, nomeadamente os clássicos, e antologias que incluíam vários autores japoneses antigos – e obras mais contemporâneas, principalmente em inglês. Li também alguma poesia chinesa, de que os poetas japoneses clássicos eram grandes conhecedores.

Como li num dos textos, um haiku é uma breve imagem, um instantâneo, de um acontecimento belo ou poético ou estranho ou humorístico, ou até mesmo uma pequena pérola de conhecimento ou sabedoria da vida.

As minhas primeiras incursões neste tipo de composição datam de um muito breve período em 2009/2010, mas, por razões que também não recordo, não voltei a pensar no assunto. Por altura do fim do verão de 2017, quando andava a ler um livro de uma poetisa portuguesa, algo voltou a despertar em mim e dei comigo de novo a compor haikus com alguma frequência.

Na composição dos meus haikus usei as regras que aprendi nas introduções de alguns dos livros, nomeadamente a golden rule das 5-7-5 sílabas em 3 versos, em linguagem do dia-a-dia, sem rima. Na contagem de sílabas utilizei o método que é comum em poesia, como a contagem de uma vogal que se segue a uma vogal no fim de uma palavra como fazendo parte da sílaba anterior, e para a contagem total das sílabas de um verso por vezes usar a última sílaba tónica. Como será fácil de perceber, nem sempre fui muito rigorosa nesta contagem, a bem da harmonia poética – ou foi o que me pareceu na altura em que os compus.

Como o japonês é uma língua em que não existem letras maiúsculas, convencionou-se que os versos dos haikus comecem todos com minúsculas. Foi o que fiz, mas optei por manter o "I" inglês e os substantivos em alemão.

Quanto aos temas, comecei pelo que tradicionalmente era feito, a descrever as pequenas maravilhas da Natureza, mas depois, sem propriamente ter consciência dessa extensão, comecei a compor haikus que relatavam acontecimentos, pensamentos, desejos, dúvidas, mesmo pequenas sentenças filosóficas sobre a vida humana em geral e a minha em particular.

A certa altura, lembrei-me de traduzir para inglês um dos haikus, e achei que também tinha um toque poético. Tive então a ideia de traduzir os meus haikus para as línguas que conheço. E achei o resultado fascinante – não só soavam bem nas outras línguas, como com alguma frequência, estranhamente ou não, a contagem das sílabas não ia muito fora do cânone, ocasionalmente com apenas ligeiros retoques. O inglês raramente precisou de apoio externo, mas como não sou tão fluente em alemão, francês e espanhol, pedi a correção por pessoas com mais conhecimentos destas línguas, preferencialmente naturais dos países em questão.

Recentemente pensei reunir todos os meus haikus num livro, arrumados por ordem cronológica.

Nalguns casos senti a necessidade de registar algum contexto para tornar mais compreensivos alguns dos haikus, o que não é ideia original mas que encontrei nas antologias de autores clássicos, e que me pareceu ser útil por vezes. Outras questões de que me apercebi à medida que ia tendo mais conhecimentos, é a de que os haikus são com frequência carregados de simbologia oriental que nos escapa, de jogo com os diferentes sentidos das palavras, e também muitas vezes inspirados em poesia antiga, tanto chinesa como japonesa, algo que igualmente não aprendi a fazer. Um apontamento final importante: como nunca aprendi numa escola, ou tive alguém mais conhecedor a ensinar-me, muitos erros certamente cometi, e bastantes destes haikus nem sequer o serão verdadeiramente. Mas, mesmo não sendo verdadeiros haikus, poderão, talvez, ser considerados pequenos fragmentos poéticos.

## Foreword

I don't exactly recall when or where I first came to read the form of Japanese poetry called haiku, but it immediately interested me. I found it beautiful and poetic and, at least on the surface, simple. It pleased me also because haiku is a "condensed", telegraphic form of expression, much like my own way of seeing and organizing the world. It was created as a poetry of nature, so different from the wordy, intellectual, political and sex driven Western poetry. I don't intend to minimize the beauty achieved by the poets of the civilization in which I was born but the lightness of haikus is very special to me.

A haiku is a brief image, a snapshot, of a poetical or beautiful, a strange or funny or even a small pearl of knowledge or wisdom of life.

It is rather fascinating that a poetic form, created more than 400 years ago, in a time, culture, language, and writing so different from ours can sound beautifully after a transposition to the Western languages. And more than that allow haikus to be created in every language, maintaining their original charm.

To write the haikus I used the traditional rules (which are not exactly consensual amongst its authors), namely the form 5-7-5 syllables in three verses, using everyday language, without rime. I counted the syllables as it is generally used in poetry, as counting a vowel after a word that finishes with a vowel as the same, and to count the syllables in each line using the last stressed one. As it is easily seen, I have sometimes not used these rules strictly, for the sake of poetic harmony, or so I thought then.

As there are no capital letters in the Japanese language, it was agreed that all the verses in the haikus start with small letters. That is how I did but decided to keep the "I" in English and the nouns in German.

As for themes, initially I started by the classic ones, that describe the little wonders of Nature, but soon, without being really aware of it, I started to compose haikus that described what happened to me, thoughts, wishes, doubts, even philosophical ideas about human life in general and my own.

At some point I had the idea of transposing my haikus to English first, then to German, French and Spanish, and found the result fascinating: not only they sounded nice in those languages, but also on many occasions the number of syllables was not that different from the original, while at other times they only needed a little retouch, eventually maintaining meaning over metrics. The haikus in this book are in chronological order as they were written. Many famous and less famous authors all over the world have written haikus in different layouts. And it is totally acceptable, for the sake of poetry.

**Primeiros Haikus**

[dezembro/janeiro 2009/2010]

1.

    sobre as pedras
    o rio saltita, canta
    tão cristalino

2.

    uma folha cai
    no silêncio pardo
    duma floresta

3.

    uma pequena flor
    desperta a floresta
    adormecida

4.

    a chuva fria
    bate naquela janela
    e faz-me sorrir

5.

    o frio lá fora
    e eu quentinha
    a lenha arde

6.

    da vida só sei
    as mais pequenas coisas
    alma sem visão

7.

    não acredito
    no amor absoluto
    e tenho pena

**Haikus recentes**

[a partir de agosto 2017]

8.

gaivotas piando
o mar ao longe, azul e verde
o verão é bom!

9.

o vento sopra
agitando as árvores e as almas
a vida é assim

[escritos num fim de tarde de agosto enquanto esperava o transporte depois da diálise, na clínica perto do rio]

10.

na fresca manhã
grito de gaivota ao longe
som-odor de mar

11.

ainda mais forte
o vento bate na janela
adeus ao sono

[escritos de manhã muito cedo, quando tentava dormir mais um pouco]

\* \* \*

12.

a imagem diz tudo
palavras de pouco servem
mas ninguém se cala

\* \* \*

13.

vi um colibri
beijar uma flor na janela
mágico instante!

[escrito quando me lembrei daquela altura em que vi um colibri na floreira da janela da cozinha da minha irmã em Grand Rapids, em julho 2016]

\* \* \*

14.

cheiro a palha
vastas planícies douradas
verão além tejo

[escrito numa viagem de regresso do Alentejo]

15.

no céu de verão
pássaros planam na brisa
leves e livres

*in the summer sky*
*birds glide in the breeze*
*so light, strong and free*

[primeira tradução em inglês]

16.

viver é duro
e sempre curto demais
mas há beleza!

*to live is so hard*
*and always our time is short*
*but there´s beauty!*

17.

grito súbito
uma vida que nasce
e logo acaba

*a sudden loud cry*
*a human life is born*
*and then all is over*

18.

soldado de barro
sanguinário foi teu tempo
de vida e tua morte

*soldier of clay*
*the bloody past you´ve seen*
*and the way you died*

[escrito por altura da exposição de soldados de terracota do imperador chinês]

19.

o fogo grassa –
à sua passagem devora
o nosso futuro

[escrito durante os terríveis incêndios do verão de 2017 que destruíram grande parte das florestas nacionais e nos quais mais de cem pessoas morreram]

3

20.

    sensação de sede
    ao olhar a planura seca
    é o alentejo

21.

    árvores em fila
    no amplo campo seco
    sinal de água

    *trees in a straight line*
    *on the wide yellow field*
    *proof of a small river*

22.

    devagar inspiro
    o ar que vem da janela
    aromas de verão...

    *slowly I inhale*
    *the air coming from the window*
    *smells of the summer...*

* * *

23.

    noite em claro
    como se agarra o sono
    que não quer chegar?

24.

    noite a acabar
    com luz e sons do novo dia
    fim do silêncio

25.

    noite sem estrelas
    a bruma tudo cobre
    de um branco espesso

26.

odor a maresia
instinto primordial
origem da vida

[o cheiro a maresia sempre derpertou em mim um instinto de pertença e comunhão com o mar]

27.

tempo mais fresco
o ciclo da natureza
roda sem parar

28.

não há cegonhas
os ninhos estão vazios
mau tempo virá

*I see not one stork*
*all the nests are empty*
*bad weather will come*

29.

as andorinhas
e as cegonhas foram-se
inverno a chegar

[no outono houve uma altura em que não víamos cegonhas quando íamos ao Alentejo, o que nos fez pensar que as cegonhas teriam antecipado mau tempo e teriam migrado em maior quantidade que habitualmente, o que depois não aconteceu]

\* \* \*

30.

viver é sofrer
em tudo se manifesta
mas vale a pena...

[escrito antes de uma sessão de diálise...]

\* \* \*

31.

o ribeiro corre
canta nas pedras frias
brilha ao sol/luar

32.

velho moinho
quanta farinha moeste
no teu passado?

33.

o sol abrasa
a planície dourada,
cheiro a palha

34.

choveu de manhã
que bom odor a terra molhada
e eucalipto

* * *

35.

sou uma borboleta
esvoaçando insegura
num tempo roubado

[escrito durante uma sessão de diálise, ao pensar na minha magreza e fragilidade, e esta realidade de ter uma vida artificialmente prolongada]

* * *

36.

tapete de folhas
a estalar sob os meus pés
outono já é

*carpet of leaves*
*popping under my two feet*
*autumn already*

37.

finalmente hoje
caiu uma chuva breve
o ar mais fresco

*finally today*
*we had a brief rain shower*
*the air is cooler*

38.

sobreiro amigo
és pródigo com os humanos
gratos pela cortiça

*cork tree our friend*
*you´re generous with humans*
*thanks for the light cork*


39.

o verde é belo
frescura e pureza
na natureza

*green is beautiful*
*freshness and purity*
*of nature*


40.

por fim a chuva cai
na terra ressequida –
há vida de novo!

*at last the rain falls*
*on the barren dry land –*
*life thrives again!*

*endlich fällt der Regen*
*auf die ausgedörrte Erde –*
*da ist wieder Leben!*

*enfin la pluie tombe*
*sur la terre si séche –*
*la vie revient!*

*por fin la lluvia cae*
*sobre la tierra seca –*
*la vida renace*

41.

as estrelas brilham
na noite fria e escura
inverno a chegar

*the stars shine*
*over the dark and cold night*
*winter is coming*

*Sterne am Himmel scheinen*
*die kalte und dunkle Nacht*
*der Winter kommt*

*les étoiles brillent*
*dans la nuit sombre et froide*
*l'hiver qui arrive*

*las estrellas brillan*
*en la noche negra y fria*
*invierno  llegando*

42.

o dia amanheceu
está sol mas vento frio
custa a levantar

*already it´s day time*
*the sun is up but cold wind*
*it´s hard to get up*

*Tageslicht dämmerte*
*es ist sonnig, aber der kalte Wind*
*erhebt sich schwer*

*le jour commence*
*il fait soleil mais vent froid*
*dur de se lever*

*rompendo el dia*
*sol y viento frio*
*duro es despertar*

43.

não digo nada
aceitar esta vida
é o meu segredo

*I do not say anything*
*to accept this way of life*
*is my secret*

*ich sage nichts*
*akzeptiere dieses Leben*
*es ist meines Geheimnis*

*je ne dis rien*
*accepter cette vie*
*est mon secret*

*no digo nada*
*aceptar esta vida*
*es mi secreto*

[escrito numa sessão de diálise]


44.

a gaivota piou
na manhã fria e húmida
pensei em mar azul

*the seagull cried loud*
*in the cold and damp morning*
*I thought of blue sea*

*die Möwe schrie*
*an einem kalten, feuchten Morgen*
*ich dachte an blaues Meer*

*une mouette a crié*
*dans le matin froid et humide*
*je pense à la mer bleue*

*pió la gaviota*
*en la fria y húmeda mañana*
*pensé en el mar azul*

* * *

9

45.

a noite é longa
e o sono que não chega
manhã já a nascer

*the night is very long*
*sleep that doesn´t come*
*morning already*


46.

a vida tem dor sim
mas também amor e pasmo
aproveita-a bem!

*life has lots of pain*
*but also love and wonder*
*enjoy it well enough!*


47.

o que importa
nesta breve vida aqui
é apenas o amor

*what really matters*
*in this short life here*
*it is only love*

*was zählt*
*in diesem kurzen Leben hier*
*es ist nur die Liebe*

*ce qui importe*
*dans cette courte vie ici*
*c´est seulement l´amour*

*que importa*
*en esta vida breve*
*solo el amor*

48.

chove há horas
o vento sopra furioso
e eu sem dormir

*for a long time it rains*
*the wind blows furiously*
*and I cannot sleep*

*es hat stundenlang geregnet*
*der Wind weht wütend*
*und ich schlafe nicht*

*la pluie tombe fort*
*le vent souffle rageux*
*et moi qui ne dors plus*

*hace horas que llueve*
*el viento sopla con furia*
*y yo sin dormir*

\* \* \*

49.

certeza do fim
é a constante da vida
a não esquecer

*assurance of an end*
*is the constant of life*
*never to be forgotten*

*Gewissheit des Endes*
*ist eine Konstante des Lebens*
*nicht zu vergessen*

*assurance de sa fin*
*c´est la constante de la vie*
*à ne pas oublier*

*certeza del final*
*es la constante de la vida*
*que no puedes olvidar*

50.

o amor pode ser
tanta coisa diferente
mas sempre espanto

*love can be*
*so many diferent things*
*but always wonder*

*Liebe kann*
*so viele verschiedene Dinge sein*
*aber immer wieder Erstaunen*

*l´amour peut être*
*tant de choses différentes*
*mais toujours étonnement*

*el amor puede ser*
*tantas cosas distintas*
*pero siempre assombro*

51.

triste é a velhice
o corpo dói e está pesado
a mente cansada

*old age is so sad*
*the body hurts and feels heavy*
*the mind so tired*

*traurig ist das Alter*
*der Körper tut veh und der schwere*
*Verstand ist müde*

*triste est la vieillesse*
*le corps fait mal et est lourd*
*l´esprit fatigué*

*triste es la vejez*
*el cuerpo duele y pesa*
*la mente cansada*

\* \* \*

52.

pássaro cantas
trinados e harmonias
pura beleza

*bird, you sing*
*warbles and harmonies*
*pure beauty*

*Vogel, du da singst*
*zwitschernd und harmonisch*
*pure Schönheit*

*oiseau tu chantes*
*trilles et harmonies*
*pure beauté*

*pájaro cantas*
*trinos y harmonias*
*pura belleza*

53.

ruínas ao longe
memórias de um passado
já esquecido

*ruins in the distance*
*memories of a past*
*long forgotten*

*Ruinen in der Ferne*
*Erinnerungen an die Vergangenheit*
*schon vergessen*

*ruines au loin*
*mémoires d´un passé*
*déjà oublié*

*ruinas a lo lejos*
*memorias de un passado*
*ya olvidado*

54.

reflexo no vidro
velha mulher, ar cansado
percebo que sou eu

*window reflection*
*an old woman, looking tired*
*it´s only me*

*Spiegelung im Glas*
*alte Frau, die müde aussieht*
*ich erkenne, dass ich es bin*

*reflet sur le verre*
*vieille femme, l´air fatigué*
*je réalise que c´est moi*

*reflejo en el cristal*
*vieja mujer, semblante cansada*
*percibo que soy yo*

55.

silêncio na noite
quando todos já dormem
e eu acordada

*silence in the night*
*when everybody is asleep*
*only I am awake*

*Stille in der Nacht*
*wenn alle schlafen*
*und ich bin wach*

*silence dans la nuit*
*quand tous sont endormis*
*et moi réveillée*

*silencio en la noche*
*quando todos duermen*
*y yo despierta*

* * *

56.

todos corremos
sem parar até morrer
e não há mais nada

*we all run so fast*
*nonstop till we die*
*and there´s nothing more*

*wir laufen alle*
*ohne aufzuhören, bis wir sterben*
*und es ist nicht mehr übrig*

*nous courons tous*
*sans arrêt vers la mort*
*et il n´y a rien de plus*

*todos corremos*
*sin parar hasta morir*
*y no hay nada más*

\* \* \*

57.

gosto desta planta
do tempo da minha mãe
memórias dela

[escrito num dia em que tratava das minhas plantas e reparei numa em
particular, que está há tantos anos na minha cozinha]

*I really like this plant*
*from back when my mother was alive*
*strong memories of her*

*ich mag diese Pflanze*
*aus der Zeit meiner Mutter*
*Erinnerungen an sie*

*cette plante me plaît*
*du temps où ma mère vivait*
*souvenirs d´elle*

*me gusta esta planta*
*del tiempo en que vivía mi madre*
*recuerdos de ella*

58.

adoro o silêncio
da noite quando todos dormem
momentos de paz

*I just love the silence*
*at night when everybody sleeps*
*moments of real peace*

*ich liebe die Stille*
*der Nacht wenn alle schlafen*
*Momente des Friedens*

*j´adore le silence*
*de la nuit quand tous dorment*
*moments de vraie paix*

*adoro el silencio*
*de la noche cuando todos duermen*
*momentos de tranquilidad*

59.

verão de novo
dias longos cheios de luz
apetece cantar/dançar/amar/voar!

[como não consegui escolher definitivamente nenhuma das opções, resolvi deixá-las todas, para selecionar no momento... Escrito num dia frio de inverno a sonhar com o verão!]

*summer again*
*clear long sunny days*
*feels like singing/dancing/loving/flying!*

*Sommer wieder*
*lange Tage voller Licht*
*wilst du singen/tanzen/lieben/fliegen!*

*été qui revient*
*de longues journées pleines de lumière*
*on a envie de chanter/danser/aimer/voler!*

*verano de nuevo*
*días largos llenos de luz*
*apetece cantar/bailar/amar/volar!*

60.

os dias passam
com uma rapidez louca
e logo é o fim

*our days go by*
*with enormous speed*
*and soon comes the end*

*die Tage vergehen*
*mit verrükter Geshwindigkeit*
*und bald ist das Ende*

*les jours passent*
*avec une vitesse folle*
*et bientôt c´est la fin*

*los dias pasan*
*con loca velocidad*
*y luego el fin*

61.

que posso fazer
para aproveitar melhor
a vida que resta?

*what can I do*
*to better enjoy*
*my remaining life?*

*was kann ich machen*
*um das beste daraus zu machen*
*das Leben, das bleibt?*

*que puis-je faire*
*pour profiter au maximum*
*de la vie qui me reste?*

*que puedo hacer*
*para aprovechar mejor*
*la vida que me queda?*

62.

não é mistério
apenas a realidade
a vida que temos

*it´s no mistery*
*just the reality*
*this life we lead*

*es ist kein Geheiminis*
*einfach die Realität*
*das Leben, das wir haben*

*ce n´est pas un mystère*
*juste la réalité*
*la vie que nous avons*

*no es mistério*
*sólo la realidad*
*la vida que tenemos*

* * *

63.

finalmente chove
a natureza cedeu
e cuida de nós

*strong rain at last*
*mother nature gave in*
*and takes care of us*

*endlich regnet es*
*di Natur ist weg*
*und passt auf uns auf*

*enfin il pleut*
*la nature a cédé*
*et prend soin de nous*

*finalmente llueve*
*la naturaleza cedió*
*y cuida de nosotros*

64.

com tanta chuva
tudo verde, florido
a vida renasce!

*with so much rain*
*all is green, all is blooming*
*life is reborn!*

*der viele Regen*
*alles grün, blumig*
*das Leben ist wiedergeboren*

*avec tant de pluie*
*tout est vert, fleuri*
*la vie renaît!*

*con tanta lluvia*
*todo verde, florido*
*la vida renace!*

\* \* \*

65.

não tenho medo
a morte é tão natural
mas gosto da vida

*I am not affraid*
*death is really so natural*
*but I like living*

*ich habe keine Angst*
*der Tod ist so natürlich*
*aber ich lebe gerne*

*je n´ai pas peur*
*la mort est si naturelle*
*mais j´aime vivre*

*no tengo miedo*
*la muerte es tan natural*
*pero me gusta la vida*

\* \* \*

66.

que agradável é
sentir de novo no ar
o odor a flores!

*how joyfull it is*
*to feel again in the air*
*the scent of flowers!*

*wie angenehm es ist*
*wieder die Luft zu spüren*
*der Duft der Blumen!*

*c´est agréable*
*de sentir à nouveau dans l´air*
*l´odeur des fleurs*

*que agradable es*
*sentir de nuevo en el aire*
*el olor de las flores!*

67.

o jasmim que trouxe
dá perfume à casa toda
dá alegria ao lar

*the jasmine I brought*
*gives perfume to the whole house*
*and joy to the home*

*Jasmin, den du mitgebracht hast*
*parfümiert das ganze Haus*
*bringt Freude ins Haus*

*le jasmin que j´ai apporté*
*donne du parfum à toute la maison*
*de la joie au foyer*

*el jasmín que traje*
*perfuma toda la casa*
*le da alegría al hogar*

\* \* \*

68.

tenho o direito
de ser feliz se no mundo
se sofre tanto?

[escrito ao ver as notícias sobre a terrível e interminável guerra na Síria, e lembrado também dos problemas crónicos de violência, guerra e miséria em todo o mundo]

*do I have the right*
*to be happy in this world*
*of so much suffering?*

*Ich habe das Recht*
*in der Welt glücklisch sein*
*leiden sie so viel?*

*ai-je le droit*
*d´être heureuse si dans ce monde*
*on souffre autant?*

*tengo el derecho*
*de ser feliz si en el mundo*
*se sufre tanto?*

\* \* \*

69.

respirar fundo
sentir das flores o odor
grata pela vida

*breathing deep*
*feeling the smell of flowers*
*grateful for life*

*einen tiefen Atemzug nehmen*
*die Blumen riechen*
*dankbar für das Leben*

*respirer profondément*
*sentir l´odeur des fleurs*
*merci à la vie*

*respirar hondo*
*sentir de las flores el odor*
*grata por la vida*

21

70.

fico bem feliz
de ouvir chuva forte cair
este ano temos água

*I´m really happy*
*to hear the strong rain falling*
*there´ll be water this year*

*ich bin so glücklich*
*starken Regen fallen zu hören*
*dieses Jahr haben wir Wasser*

*je suis bien heureuse*
*d'entendre tant de pluie tomber*
*cet année on a de l´eau*

*me siento muy feliz*
*de oír la lluvia fuerte*
*este año tenemos agua*

71.

o vento forte
arrasta árvores e telhados
enfurece o mar

[sobre as terríveis tempestades que têm assolado o país neste inverno tardio de
2018]

*the strong wind*
*drags trees and roofs*
*enrages the sea*

*der starke Wind*
*fegt Bäume und Dächer weg*
*tobt das Meer*

*le vent fort*
*arrache les arbres et les toits*
*fait enrager la mer*

*el viento fuerte*
*arrastra árboles y techos*
*enfurece el mar*

\* \* \*

22

72.

sonhei criar
algo de belo e útil
mas a veia é fraca

> I dreamt of creating
> something beautiful and useful
> but the talent is weak

ich träumte davon,
etwas Schönes und Nützliches zu erschaffen
aber die Ader ist schwach

> j´ai rêvé de créer
> quelque chose de beau et d´utile
> mais le talent est faible

> soñe crear
> algo de bello e útil
> pero la vena es débil

* * *

73.

as asas transparentes
a libelinha passa voando
sobre o meu lago

> transparent wings
> the dragonfly flies by
> over my small pond

> den transparenten Flügeln
> die Libelle fliegt vorbei
> über meinen Teich

> ailes transparentes
> la libellule vole
> au dessus de mon étang

> las alas transparentes
> la libélula pasa volando
> de sobre mi lago

74.

vento nos pinheiros
cheiro doce a seiva
o pinhal tão verde!

*wind in the pines*
*it smells of sweet sour sap*
*the pine forest so green*

*Wind in den Kiefern*
*süßer Geruch von Saft*
*der Tannenwald so grün!*

*vent dans les pins*
*odeur douce de la sève*
*la forêt si verte!*

*viento en los pinos*
*olor dulce de la savia*
*el pinar tan verde!*

\* \* \*

75.

silêncio profundo
nas noites da casa da praia
paraíso na terra

*deep silence*
*on the beach house nights*
*paradise on earth*

*tiefe Stille*
*in den Nächten des Strandhauses*
*das Paradies auf Erden*

*silence profond*
*dans les nuits de la maison de la plage*
*paradis sur terre*

*silencio profundo*
*el las noches de la casa de la playa*
*paraíso en la tierra*

76.

teia de aranha
brilha sob o orvalho
da fresca manhã

*spider´s web*
*glows under the dew*
*of the fresh morning*

*Spinnennetz*
*glänzt unter dem Tau*
*des kühlen Morgens*

*toile d´araignée*
*brille sous la rosée*
*de la fraîche matinée*

*tela de araña*
*brilla bajo el rocío*
*de la fria mañana*

77.

o corvo negro
enorme, à beira da estrada
esvoaça e grasna

*the black crow*
*huge, by the side of the road*
*flutters and squawks*

*die schwarze Krähe*
*riesig, am Sraßenrand*
*flattert und krächtz*

*le corbeau noir*
*immense, au bord de la route*
*bat des ailes et croasse*

*el cuervo negro*
*enorme, al borde de la carretera*
*aleata y grazna*

\* \* \*

78.

devo ser louca
ser doente e mesmo assim
apreciar a vida

*I must be crazy*
*being so sick and even so*
*enjoy living*

*ich muss verrükt sein*
*krank sein und doch*
*das Leben genießen*

*je dois être folle*
*être malade et tout de même*
*apprécier la vie*

*debo ser loca*
*ser enferma y aún así*
*apreciar la vida*

\* \* \*

79.

se há solução
para salvar o mundo, só
se todos o amarmos

[quando reli este haiku depois de o escrever, soou a *slogan* de uma organização ambientalista]

*if there´s a solution*
*to save the world, it´s*
*all of us loving it*

*ob es eine Lösung gibt*
*um die Welt zu retten, nur*
*wenn wir sie alle lieben*

*s´il y a une solution*
*pour sauver notre monde,*
*si nous l'aimons tous*

*si hay solución*
*para salvar al mundo,*
*es que todos lo amemos*

26

* * *

80.

este corpo frágil
agarra-se à vida
apesar de tudo

*this fragile body*
*clings to life*
*in spite of everything*

*dieser zerbrechliche Körper*
*klammert sich an das Leben*
*schließlich*

*ce corps fragile*
*s'accroche à la vie*
*malgré tout*

*este cuerpo frágil*
*aferrasse a la vida*
*a pesar de todo*

81.

o passado vai
bem longe, e no entanto
rege as nossas vidas

*the past is gone*
*far away, and yet*
*still rules our lives*

*die Vergangenheit geht*
*weit veg und doch*
*regelt sie unser Leben*

*le passé est loin*
*trés loin, et pourtant*
*règle nos vies*

*el passado va*
*muy lejos, y sin embargo*
*regla nuestras vidas*

82.

se há amor total
e nem sempre o será
é o amor de mãe

*if total love exists*
*and it´s not always the case*
*it´s a mother´s love*

*wenn ist totale Liebe gibt*
*und das wird nicht immer so sein*
*Ist es die Liebe einer Mutter*

*s´il y a un amour total*
*et ce ne sera pas toujours le cas*
*c´est l´amour maternel*

*si hay amor total*
*y no sempre lo sera*
*es el amor de madre*

* * *

83.

jovens soldados
que montam belos cavalos
visão do passado

[ao ver no caminho para a diálise dois cavalos enormes e bonitos montados por
guardas republicanos, como os que passavam quase diariamente à nossa porta
no bairro da Ajuda na minha infância]

*young soldiers*
*riding beautiful horses*
*vision of the past*

*junge Soldaten*
*die schöne Pferde reiten*
*Vision der Vergangenheit*

*jeunes soldats*
*qui montent de beaux chevaux*
*vision du passé*

*jovenes soldados*
*que montan hermosos caballos*
*visión del passado*

84.

chove de novo
colho uma gota com a língua
o sabor é doce

> *it´s raining again*
> *I take a drop on my tongue*
> *it tastes sweet*

> *es regnet wieder*
> *ich zeichne einen Tropfen auf meine Zunge*
> *der Geschmack ist süß*

> *il pleut encore*
> *je reçois une goutte sur la langue*
> *le goût est doux*

> *llueve de nuevo*
> *cojo una gota con la lengua*
> *el sabor es dulce*

> * * *

85.

há sempre sempre
tanto para fazer e sem tempo
para respirar!

> *always always*
> *so much to do and no time*
> *to breathe!*

> *es gibt immer, immer*
> *so viel zu tun und keine Zeit*
> *zu atmen!*

> *Il y a toujours toujours*
> *tant de choses à faire et pas de temps*
> *de respirer!*

> *siempre hay siempre*
> *tanto que hacer y sin tiempo*
> *para respirar!*

86.

a minha mente
pode imaginar tudo
não é real... mas é bom

*my mind*
*can imagine anything*
*it´s not real... but it is good*

*mein Geist*
*kann sich alles vorstellen*
*es ist nicht echt... aber gut*

*mon esprit*
*peut tout imaginer*
*ce n´est pas réel... mais c´est bon*

*mi mente*
*puede imaginarse-lo todo*
*no es real... pero es bueno*

\* \* \*

87.

fecho os olhos
ouço pássaros cantar
é primavera!

*I shut my eyes*
*and hear the birds singing*
*it´s spring again!*

*ich schließe meine Augen*
*ich höre Vögel singen*
*es ist wieder Frühling!*

*je ferme les yeux*
*j´entends les oiseaux chanter*
*c´est le printemps!*

*cierro los ojos*
*oigo los pájaros cantar*
*es primavera!*

88.

criança que fui
botão pleno de futuro
e que acabou assim...

*little child I was*
*bud with a full future*
*and that ended like this...*

*Kind, zu dem ich ging*
*Volle zukünftige Taste*
*und es endete so...*

*enfant que j´étais*
*bourgeon plein d'avenir*
*et qui a fini comme ça...*

*niña que era*
*botón lleno de futuro*
*y se terminó así...*

89.

desejei viver
sem deixar qualquer marca
nenhuma memória

*I wished I would live*
*without leaving any mark*
*no memory*

*ich wollte leben*
*ohne irgendwelche Spuren zu hinterlassen*
*keine Erinnerung*

*je voulais vivre*
*sans laisser de marque*
*aucun souvenir*

*deseo vivir*
*sin dejar cualquier marca*
*ninguna memoria*

32

90.

a música leva-me
para outras esferas
devia ouvir mais

*music takes me*
*to other amazing worlds*
*I should listen more*

*die Musik nimmt mich*
*für andere Bereiche*
*ich hätte mehr hören sollen*

*la musique m'amène*
*vers d'autres sphères*
*je devrais en écouter plus*

*la musica me lleva*
*para otras esferas*
*debería escuchar más*

91.

cada mulher pode ser
um ser completo em si
depois vêm os outros

*each woman is*
*a complete being in herself*
*then the others can come in*

*jede Frau ist*
*ein selbst vollständiges Wesen*
*dann kommen die anderen*

*chaque femme peut être*
*un être complet en soi*
*puis viennent les autres*

*cada mujer es*
*un ser completo en sí mismo*
*despues vienen los demás*

\* \* \*

92.

instante da aurora
em que o tempo para –
breve magia

*moment of the dawn*
*when time stops –*
*brief magic*

*Augenblick der Morgendämmerung*
*wenn die Zeit stehen bleibt –*
*kurze Magie*

*moment de l´aube*
*quand le temps s´arrête –*
*brève magie*

*instante de la aurora*
*en que el tiempo se para –*
*breve magia*

93.

a noite passou
já o passarinho canta
na minha cozinha

*the night has passed*
*already the little bird sings*
*in my kitchen*

*die Nacht verging*
*schon singt der Vogel*
*in meiner Küche*

*la nuit est passée*
*déjà le petit oiseau chante*
*dans ma cuisine*

*la noche passó*
*ya el pájaro canta*
*en mi cocina*

* * *

94.

que estranho é
ouvir os meus pensamentos
mas nada de som

*how strange it is*
*to listen to my own thoughts*
*and hear no sound*

*wie seltsam es ist*
*meine Gedanken zu hören*
*aber kein Ton*

*comme c´est étrange*
*d´écouter mes pensées*
*mais aucun son*

*que estraño es*
*oír mis pensamientos*
*y ningún sonido*

\* \* \*

95.

que tristeza é
a sede que temos
e nada consegue aplacar

[sobre a sede que os doentes de diálise têm sempre, devido à restrição de líquidos]

how sad it is
the thirst we have and nothing
can really relieve

wie traurig das ist
den Durst, den wir haben und nichts
kann man auslöschen

que c´est triste
la soif que nous avons et rien
peut l' apaiser

qué tristeza es
la sed que tenemos y nada
consigue aplacar

96.

alguma vez viste
uma rosa sem espinhos?
é porque não existe

have you ever seen
a rose without thorns?
It´s because it doesn´t exist

hast du jemals
eine Rose ohne Dornen gesehen?
weil sie es nicht gibt

avez vous déjà vu
une rose sans épines?
c´est parce que ça n´existe pas

alguna vez has visto
una rosa sin espinos?
es porque no existe

97.

já o autor disse
dormir, dormir mais que viver
nem sempre é verdade...

[sobre uma frase famosa de Baudelaire em *Les fleurs du mal - As Flores do Mal*:
"Dormir, dormir plutôt que vivre"]

*the author said
sleep, sleep, more than to live
it´s not always true...*

*schon der Autor sagte
schlafen, aber mehr zu schlafen als zu leben
ist nicht immer wahr...*

*l´auteur a dit
dormir, dormir plutôt que vivre
ce n´est pas toujours vrai...*

*el autor dijo
dormir, dormir, más que vivir
no siempre es verdad...*

\* \* \*

98.

sobre a catedral
as cegonhas majestosas
voam rumo ao sul

[referência a uma observação minha da migração das cegonhas para sul, num mês de setembro, quando visitávamos a Catedral de Sta. Sofia em Istambul]

*over the cathedral*
*the majestic storks*
*fly towards the south*

*über die Kathedrale*
*die majestätischen Störche*
*sie fliegen nach Süden*

*au-dessous de la cathédrale*
*les majestueuses cigognes*
*volent vers le sud*

*por encima de la catedral*
*las cigueñas majestuosas*
*vuelen hacia el sur*

99.

bamboleante,
lento, o camelo vai seguro
na seca paisagem

*swaying,*
*slow, the camel walks steadily*
*in the dry landscape*

*schwankend,*
*langsam geht das Kamel sicher*
*in der trockenen Landschaft*

*en se dandinant,*
*lent, le chameau marche en sécurité*
*dans le paysage sec*

*balanceante*
*lento, el camello va seguro*
*en el paisaje seco*

100.

a noite caiu
já se ouvem as garças
no canavial

*night has fallen
already the herons can be heard
over the reed*

*die Nacht ist hereingebrochen
die Reiher sind bereits zu hören
auf dem Zuckerrohrfeld*

*la nuit est tombée
on peut déjà entendre les hérons
dans le champ de canne*

*la noche cayó
ya se oyen las garzas
en el cañaveral*

101.

no fim de tarde
frente ao sol poente
gaivotas planando

*in the late afternoon
facing the setting sun
seagulls gliding*

*am späten Nachmittag
mit Blick auf die untergehende Sonne
Möwen gleiten*

*en fin d´après-midi
face au soleil couchant
les mouettes plannent*

*en el fin de tarde
frente al sol poniente
gaviotas planando*

\* \* \*

102.

indiferente
o relógio do tempo
roda sem parar

*indifferent*
*the time clock wheels*
*without stopping*

*gleichgültig*
*die Zeithur*
*dreht, ohne anzuhalten*

*indifférent*
*l'horloge du temps*
*tourne sans s'arrêter*

*indiferente*
*el reloj del tiempo*
*rueda sin parar*

\* \* \*

103.

crinas ao vento
cascos martelam o chão
cavalos voando

*horsehair in the wind*
*hooves hammer the ground*
*horses flying*

*Mähnen im Wind*
*Hufe stampfen auf den Boden*
*fliegende Pferde*

*crin de cheval dans le vent*
*les sabots martèlent le sol*
*chevaux volants*

*crines al viento*
*los cascos martillan el suelo*
*caballos volando*

104.

parece chover
na janela ouço cair
chuva redentora!

*it seems it´s raining*
*on the window I hear falling*
*redemptive rain!*

*es scheint zu regnen*
*am Fenster höre ich den*
*erlösender Regen fallen!*

*il semble pleuvoir*
*sur la fenêtre j´entends tomber*
*la pluie rédemptrice!*

*parece llover*
*en la ventana oigo caer*
*lluvia redentora!*

105.

já madrugada!
cheia de frio e sono
duro dia me espera

[escrito quando acordei, num dia de diálise, ainda inverno]

*dawn already!*
*feeling cold and sleepy*
*hard day awaits me*

*es ist schon Morgen!*
*voller Kälte und schäfrig*
*ein harter Tag erwartet mich*

*c´est déjà l´aube!*
*pleine de froid et de sommeil*
*une dure journée m´attend*

*ya madrugada!*
*llena de frio y sueño*
*duro día me espera*

\* \* \*

41

106.

passeios nos bosques
apanhar rãs na ribeira
memórias felizes

*walkings in the woods*
*catching frogs in the brook*
*happy memories*

*Spaziergänge im Wald*
*Frösche im Bach fangen*
*glückliche Erinnerungen*

*promenades dans les bois*
*atrapper des grenouilles dans le ruisseau*
*joyeux souvenirs*

*paseos en los bosques*
*coger ranas en el arroyo*
*memorias felices*

107.

férias na infância
lendo na tarde tranquila
o tempo parava

*holidays in childhood*
*reading in the quiet afternoons*
*time stopped*

*Ferien in der Kindheit*
*lesen am ruhigen Nachmittag*
*die Zeit ist stehen geblieben*

*vacances dans l´enfance*
*lectures dans l´après-midi tranquille*
*le temps s´arrêtait*

*vacaciones en la infancia*
*leyendo en la tarde tranquila*
*el tiempo paraba*

\* \* \*

108.

frágil coração
palpitas tanto por vezes
não pares ainda...

*fragile heart*
*you beat so fast sometimes*
*do not stop yet...*

*zerbrechliches Herz*
*du hast manchmal so viel Herzklopfen*
*hör noch nicht auf...*

*coeur fragile*
*tu bats si fort parfois*
*ne t´arrête pas encore...*

*fragil corazón*
*palpitas tanto a veces*
*no pares todavia...*

109.

o sangue vibra
no meu braço massacrado
o preço da vida...

*the blood vibrates*
*in my slain arm*
*the price of life...*

*das Blut vibriert*
*auf meinem erschlagenen Arm*
*der Preis des Lebens...*

*le sang vibre*
*dans mon bras massacré*
*le prix de la vie...*

*la sangre vibra*
*en mi brazo massacrado*
*el precio de la vida...*

110.

o meu desejo
é apagar-me sem ruído
qual vela ardida

*I really do wish*
*to end my life without noise*
*like a burned out candle*

*mein Wunsch*
*ist es, mich geräuschlos auszulöschen*
*wie eine brennende Kerze*

*mon désir*
*c´est de m´éteindre sans bruit*
*comme une bougie éteinte*

*mi deseo*
*es borrarme sin ruido*
*como qué vela ardida*

111.

pouco nesta vida
é aquilo que sonhamos –
sonhar outros sonhos!

*little in this life*
*is what we dream –*
*dream other dreams!*

*wenig in diesem Leben*
*ist das, wovon wir träumen –*
*andere Träume zu träumen!*

*peu dans cette vie*
*c´est ce que nous rêvons –*
*rêver d´autres rêves!*

*poco en esta vida*
*es lo que soñamos –*
*soñar otros sueños!*

112.

palavras, palavras
estou tão cansada delas!
preciso silêncio

*words, more words*
*I´m so tired of them!*
*I need silence*

*Wörter, Wörter*
*ich bin so müde von ihnen!*
*ich brauche Stille*

*mots, toujours mots*
*je suis si fatiguée d´eux!*
*j´ai besoin de silence*

*palabras, palabras*
*estoy tan cansada de ellas!*
*necessito silencio*

113.

tanto para fazer
tão pouco tempo de vida
é a nossa sina

*so much to do*
*so little time of life*
*it´s our fate*

*so viel zu tun*
*so wenig Zeit zum Leben*
*ist unser Schicksal*

*tants de choses à faire*
*tellement peu de temps de vie*
*c´est notre destin*

*tanto que hacer*
*tan poco tiempo de vida*
*es nuestra sina*

114.

que delícia é
uma longa noite de sono
pena ser tão raro...

*how delightful it is*
*a long night's sleep*
*too bad it's so rare...*

*was für ein Vergnügen es ist*
*eine lange Nachtruhe zu genießen*
*schade, dass es so selten ist...*

*que c'est délicieux*
*une longue nuit de sommeil*
*dommage, c'est tellement rare...*

*que delicia es*
*una larga noche de sueño*
*pena que sea tan raro...*

\* \* \*

115.

é o fio da vida
um ser que nasce de outro
a mãe e o filho

*it's the thread of life*
*a being born of another being*
*the mother and the son*

*es ist der Faden des Lebens*
*ein Wesen, das aus einem anderen geboren ist*
*Mutter und Sohn*

*c'est le fil de la vie*
*un être né d'un autre être*
*mère et fils*

*es el hilo de la vida*
*un ser que nace de otro*
*la madre y el hijo*

46

116.

ouvi a musa…
nem tudo está perdido
nas minhas insónias

*I heard the muse…*
*not everything is lost*
*in my insomnia*

*ich habe die Muse gehört…*
*nicht alles ist verloren*
*in meiner Schlaflosigkeit*

*j´ai entendu la muse…*
*tout n'est pas perdu*
*dans mes insomnies*

*oí la musa…*
*no todo está perdido*
*en mi insomnio*

117.

os ventos da vida
pregam-nos tantas partidas –
olhar em frente

*the winds of life*
*they play us so many tricks –*
*look ahead*

*die Winde des Lebens*
*sie predigen so viele Spiele –*
*vorausschauend*

*les vents de la vie*
*nous font tant de jeux –*
*regardons vers l´avenir*

*los vientos de la vida*
*tanto se burlan –*
*mirar hacia adelante*

\* \* \*

118.

a lua de prata
desenha uma estrada
no mar sereno

*the silver moon*
*draws a road*
*on the quiet sea*

*der Silbermond*
*zeichnet eine Straße*
*auf dem heiteren Meer*

*la lune d´argent*
*dessine une route*
*sur la mer tranquille*

*la luna de plata*
*dibuja una carretera*
*en el mar sereno*

\* \* \*

119.

o gato dorme
a sono solto à lareira
como o invejo!

*the cat is asleep*
*so loose by the fireplace*
*how I envy it!*

*die Katze schläft*
*am Kamin*
*wie ich sich beneide!*

*le chat dort*
*si tranquille près da la cheminée*
*comme je l´envie!*

*el gato duerme*
*sueño suelto a la chimenea*
*como le envidio!*

120.

o gato passou
olhou os peixes no lago
almoço o que viu

*the cat passed by*
*looked at the fishes in the lake*
*lunch was what it saw*

*die Katze ging vorbei*
*schaute sich die Fische im See an*
*Mittagessen, was er sah*

*le chat est passé*
*regarder les poissons dans le lac*
*il voit son déjeuner*

*el gato passó*
*miró los pesces en el lago*
*desayuno lo que vio*

\* \* \*

121.

porque só temos
a noção do que amámos
quando o perdemos?

*why do we only have*
*the notion of how much we´ve loved*
*after we´ve lost it?*

*denn wir haben nur*
*ein Gefühl für das, was wir lieben*
*wenn wir es verloren haben?*

*pourquoi avons-nous seulement*
*la notion de ce que nous avons aimé*
*quand nous le perdons?*

*porque sólo tenemos*
*la noción de lo que amamos*
*cuando lo perdimos?*

122.

deveria haver
espelhos que refletissem
almas e não rostos

*there should be*
*mirrors reflecting*
*souls and not faces*

*es sollte Spiegel geben,*
*die Seelen reflektieren*
*und nicht Gesichter*

*il devrait y avoir*
*des miroirs reflétant*
*les âmes et pas les visages*

*debería haber*
*espejos que reflejen*
*almas y no rostros*

123.

o sino da igreja
dá as horas tão alto
que acorda os mortos...

*the church bell*
*gives the hours so loud*
*that wakes up the dead...*

*die Kirchenglocke*
*sagt die Zeit so laut*
*es weckt die Toten...*

*la cloche de l´église*
*sonne les heures si fort*
*qu'elle réveille les morts...*

*la campana de la iglesia*
*da las horas tan alto*
*que despierta a los muertos...*

124.

flutuando na brisa
as bruxinhas afastam-se
tantas novas vidas


125.

mudou a hora
no início da primavera
um dia mais curto

*time change*
*in early spring*
*a shorter day*

*die Uhrzeit ändert sich*
*zu Beginn des Frühlings*
*ein kürzerer Tag*

*l´heure a changé*
*au début du printemps*
*un jour plus court*

*cambió la hora*
*al principio de la primavera*
*un dia más corto*

126.

fim de semana
dois dias de sossego que
passam a fugir...

*weekend*
*two quiet days that*
*quickly go away...*

*Wochenende*
*zwei Tage der Stille, die*
*schnell vergehen...*

*fin de la semaine*
*deux jours de calme qui*
*rapidement s´enfuient...*

*fin de semana*
*dos dias de sosiego que*
*que pasan huyendo...*

\* \* \*

127.

velho passarito
há tantos anos connosco
julguei-o eterno...

*old little bird*
*so many years with us*
*I thought it eternal...*

*altes Vögelchen*
*so viele Jahre bei uns*
*Ich dachte, es würde ewig dauern...*

*petit oiseau âgé*
*tant d´années avec nous*
*je le croyais éternel...*

*viejo pajarito*
*hace tantos años com nosotros*
*lo creí eterno...*

52

128.

tanto os meus pais
gostavam do terno bicho!
vidas passadas...

[estes dois haikus foram escritos no dia em que morreu o canário de Moçambique que eu e a minha irmã oferecemos um verão aos meus pais, há mais de 15 anos]

*both my parents*
*liked that sweet bird so much!*
*past lives...*

*beide meine Eltern*
*sie mochten den Tieranzug!*
*vergangenes Leben...*

*mes deux parents*
*aimaient beaucoup le tendre oiseau!*
*vies déjà passées...*

*Cuanto a mis padres*
*les gustaba el tierno ser!*
*vidas pasadas...*

\* \* \*

129.

como se esquecem
os horrores das guerras
e se repetem?

*how do they forget*
*the horrors of wars*
*and repeat them?*

*wie Menschen vergessen?*
*den Schrecken des Krieges*
*und sich wiederholen?*

*comment oublie-t'on*
*les horreurs des guerres*
*et elles se répètent?*

*cómo se olvidan*
*los horrores de las guerras*
*y se repiten?*

\* \* \*

130.

de novo insomne
os pequenos sons da noite
me ensurdecem

*insomniac again*
*the little sounds of the night*
*deafen me*

*wieder Schlaflosigkeit*
*die kleinen Geräusche der Nacht*
*mich betäuben*

*encore insomniaque*
*les petits bruits de la nuit*
*me rendent sourde*

*de nuevo insomne*
*los pequeños sonidos de la noche*
*me ensordecen*

131.

um ser alado
vi num sonho – ou foi ele
que sonhou comigo?

[este haiku é influência dos anjos de Rilke, poeta que andava a ler na altura em que o escrevi]

*a winged being*
*I saw in a dream – or was it*
*that dreamt of me?*

*ein geflügeltes Wesen*
*Ich sah in einem Traum – oder was es er*
*der von mir geträumt hat?*

*un être ailé*
*je l'ai vu dans un rêve – ou était-ce lui*
*qui a rêvé de moi?*

*un ser alado*
*vi en un sueño – o fue él*
*quien soñó conmigo?*

132.

estrela cadente
passou no céu estrelado
que desejo peço?...

*shooting star*
*passed in the starry sky*
*what wish shall I ask for?...*

*Sternschnuppe*
*vorbei am Sternenhimmel*
*was wünsche ich mir?...*

*étoile filante*
*est passée dans le ciel etoilé*
*quel souhait dois-je faire?...*

*estrella fugaz*
*pasó en el cielo estrellado*
*que deseo le pido?...*

133.

numa ilha grega
sonhámos viver – mas os deuses
não concordaram...

*on a greek island*
*we dreamt of living – but the gods*
*didn´t agree...*

*auf einer griechischen Insel*
*wir träumten vom Leben – aber die Götter*
*waren nicht einverstanden...*

*sur une île grecque*
*nous rêvions de vivre – mais les dieux*
*n´étaient pas d´accord...*

*en una isla griega*
*soñamos vivir – pero los dioses*
*no estuvieron de acuerdo...*

134.

para quê fugir?
fantasmas todos temos
prova que vivemos

*why run away?*
*ghosts we all have*
*proof that we lived*

*warum fliehen?*
*Geister, die wir alle haben*
*Beweis, das wir leben*

*pourquoi s´échapper?*
*les fantômes que nous avons tous*
*prouvent que nous vivons*

*para qué huir?*
*fantasmas que todos tenemos*
*prueba que vivimos*

135.

o lago do jardim
é um pequeno mundo
pleno de vida

*the garden lake*
*is a small world*
*full of life*

*der Gartenteich*
*ist eine kleine Welt*
*voller Leben*

*l'étang du jardin*
*est un tout petit monde*
*plein de vie*

*el lago del jardin*
*es un pequño mundo*
*lleno de vida*

136.

o gato saltou
filou o pássaro em voo
instinto fatal

*the cat jumped*
*caught the bird in flight*
*fatal instinct*

*die Katze sprang*
*füllte den Vogel im Flug*
*fataler Instinkt*

*le chat a sauté*
*attrapant l´oiseau en vol*
*instinct mortel*

*el gato saltó*
*atrapó el pájaro en vuelo*
*instinto fatal*

\* \* \*

137.

num dia como este
céu azul, brisa, sol morno
é bom estar vivo…

*in a day like this one*
*blue sky, breeze, warm sun*
*it's good to be alive…*

*an einem Tag wie diesem*
*blauer Himmel, Brise, warme Sonne*
*es ist gut am Leben zu sei…*

*un jour comme celui-ci*
*ciel bleu, brise, soleil chaud*
*c'est bon d'être vivant…*

*en un día como este*
*cielo azul, brisa, sol caliente*
*es bueno estar vivo…*

138.

a árvore nua
botões nas pontas dos ramos
o ciclo recomeça…

*the bare tree*
*buttons at the tip of the branches*
*the cycle resumes…*

*der nackte Baum*
*Knöpfe an den Spitzen der Zweige*
*der Zyklus wird fortgesetzt…*

*l'arbre nu*
*bourgeons au bout des branches*
*le cycle recommence…*

*el árbol desnudo*
*botones en las puntas de las ramas*
*el ciclo se reanuda…*

139.

animais estranhos
que não temem os homens
mal sabem eles...

*strange animals*
*that do not fear men*
*little do they know...*

*seltsame Tiere*
*die die Menschen nicht fürchten*
*sie ahnen nicht...*

*animaux étranges*
*qui ne craignent pas les hommes*
*comme ils savent peu...*

*animales estraños*
*que no temen a los hombres*
*mal saben ellos...*

140.

tudo tão verde
flores, perfumes no ar...
adeus inverno!

*everything so green*
*flowers, sweet scents in the air...*
*goodbye winter!*

*alles ist so grün*
*Blumen, süße Parfums in der Luft...*
*auf Wiedersehen Winter!*

*tout est si vert*
*fleurs, parfums sucrés dans l´air...*
*au revoir hiver!*

*todo tan verde*
*flores, dulces perfumes en el aire...*
*adiós invierno*

* * *

141.

cavalos nos campos
pastando erva fresca
deve saber bem...

*horses in the fields*
*grazing the fresh grass*
*it must taste good...*

*Pferde auf den Feldern*
*von weiden frischem Gras*
*sollte gut schmecken...*

*chevaux dans les champs*
*broutant de l´herbe fraîche*
*ce doit être délicieux...*

*caballos en los campos*
*patando hierba fresca*
*debe ser sabroso...*

142.

campo amarelo
são mil pequenas flores
e suaves odores...

*yellow field*
*it´s a thousand small flowers*
*and soft scents...*

*gelbes Feld*
*es gibt tausend kleine Blumen*
*und weiche Gerüche...*

*champ jaune*
*il y a un millier de petites fleurs*
*et des odeurs douces...*

*campo amarillo*
*son mil pequeñas flores*
*y suaves olores...*

143.

    fofos cordeiros
    espalhados pelo campo
    livres de novo!

        *fluffy lambs*
        *scattered across the fields*
        *free again!*

        *nette Lämmer*
        *über die Felder verstreut*
        *wieder frei!*

        *jolis agneaux*
        *éparpillés à travers les champs*
        *libres encore!*

        *lindos corderos*
        *esparcidos por los campos*
        *libres de nuevo!*

144.

    intenso perfume
    são as estevas nas bermas
    inspiro fundo

145.

    é primavera!
    uma explosão de vida
    por todo o lado!

        *it´s spring again!*
        *an explosion of life*
        *everywhere!*

        *es ist Frühling!*
        *eine Explosion des Lebens*
        *überall!*

        *c´est le printemps!*
        *une explosion de vie*
        *de tous les côtés!*

        *es primavera!*
        *una explósion de vida*
        *por todas partes!*

146.

odores do campo
nem sempre agradáveis
mas mais naturais...

*country smells*
*not always pleasant*
*but more natural...*

*Lande gerüche*
*nicht immer angenehem*
*aber natürlicher...*

*odeurs des champs*
*pas toujours agréables*
*mais plus naturelles...*

*odores del campo*
*no sempre agradables*
*pero más naturales...*

147.

ter bom olfato
é mesmo uma maldição
desligar impossível...

*having a good sense of smell*
*is really a curse*
*turn it off impossible...*

*einen guten Geruchssinn zu haben*
*ist ein Fluch*
*unmöglich abzuschalten...*

*avoir un bon odorat*
*c´est vraiment une malédiction*
*l´éteindre impossible...*

*tener buen olfato*
*es una maldición*
*desactivar impossible...*

148.

às sete, o sino
rompe o silêncio da noite
mas é domingo!

[na manhã de domingo, o sino da igreja mesmo ao lado da nossa casa, no Alentejo, o tal que "acorda os mortos", toca às sete da manhã, tal como nos outros dias todos da semana]

*at seven, the church bell*
*breaks the silence of the night*
*but it is sunday!*

*sieben Uhr, die Glocke*
*durchbricht die Stille der Nacht*
*aber es ist Sonntag!*

*à sept heures, la cloche*
*brise le silence de la nuit*
*mais c´est dimanche!*

*a las siete, la campana*
*rompe el silencio de la noche*
*pero es domingo!*

\* \* \*

149.

por mais que ouça
é sempre um milagre
o som da chuva

*how many times you hear*
*it´s always a miracle*
*the sound of rain*

*auch wenn ich noch so viel höre*
*es ist immer ein Wunder*
*das Geräusch des Regens*

*même si on l'entend souvent*
*c'est toujours un miracle*
*le bruit de la pluie*

*por más que oiga*
*es siempre un milagro*
*el sonido de la lluvia*

150.

um breve momento
de paz e felicidade –
preciosa pérola

[este haiku foi composto depois de um dia muito bom passado com o meu filho
e o meu marido, em que achei que era difícil sentir-me mais feliz do que
naqueles momentos]

*a brief moment
of peace and happiness –
precious pearl*

*ein kurzer Moment
von Frieden und Glück –
schöne Perle*

*un bref moment
de paix et de bonheur –
perle précieuse*

*un breve momento
de paz y felicidad –
preciosa perla*

\* \* \*

151.

pequena aranha
que vives na banheira
fica tranquila

[quando tínhamos na Galé a casa pequena, muitas vezes um aranhiço fazia a teia no ralo da banheira, e eu com cuidado e usando uma pá e uma vassoura pequenas, pegava nele e punha-o do lado de fora da janela, mas ele voltava e tinha de fazer o mesmo de todas as vezes que lá íamos passar o fim de semana]

*little spider*
*that lives in the bathtub*
*stay at ease*

*kleine Spinne*
*die in der Badewanne lebt*
*bewahre die Ruhe*

*petite araignée*
*qui vit dans la baignoire*
*reste tranquille*

*pequeña araña*
*que vives en la bañera*
*quédate tranquila*

\* \* \*

152.

dia tão ameno
de novo já consigo
aquecer-me ao sol

[escritos num dia depois da diálise, em que, depois de meses de frio e de chuva,
foi possível vir para a rua aquecer-me]

*such a mild day*
*again I can*
*warm up in the sun*

*so milder Tag*
*ich kann es wieder tun*
*wärme mich in der Sonne*

*journée si chaude*
*de nouveau je peux*
*me réchauffer au soleil*

*dia tan ameno*
*de nuevo ya consigo*
*calentarme al sol*

153.

o rio ao longe
novamente azul forte
sensação de paz

*the river in the distance*
*once again strong blue*
*feelings of peace*

*der Fluss in der Ferne*
*wieder stark blau*
*Gefühl des Friedens*

*la rivière au loin*
*à nouveau d´un bleu fort*
*sentiment de paix*

*el río a lo lejos*
*nuevamente azul fuerte*
*sensación de paz*

154.

primeiros rebentos
a árvore sabe que renasce
a cada ano?

[ao subir a minha rua para ir para o metro, as árvores que ainda há poucos dias tinham os ramos completamente despidos, começavam a ter lindas pequenas folhas muito verdes]

*first buds*
*does the tree know that it is reborn*
*every year?*

*erste Triebe*
*der Baum weiß, das er wiedergeboren*
*wird jedes Jahr?*

*premières pousses*
*l´arbre sait-il qu'il renaît*
*chaque année?*

*primeiros brotes*
*el árbol sabe que renace*
*a cada año?*

* * *

155.

ternos cabritinhos
brincando como cachorros
cruel é esta vida

[quando éramos crianças, a nossa avó paterna vivia na província e fazia criação de animais para consumo próprio, entre os quais havia uma cabra que todos os anos tinha um ou dois cabritos com que brincávamos, e nos seguiam pelo quintal como cachorros. A vida é cruel porque no fim do verão os cabritos eram consumidos em assado... Tal é a vida no campo!]

*little goats*
*playing like puppies*
*cruel is this life*

*kleine Ziegen*
*spielen wie kleine Hunde*
*grausam ist dieses Leben*

*petites chèvres*
*jouant comme des petits chiens*
*cruelle est cette vie*

*pequeñas cabras*
*jugando como pequeños perros*
*cruel es esta vida*

\* \* \*

156.

as rãs do meu lago
coaxam na noite cálida
são os sons do verão

*the frogs in my pond*
*ribbit in the warm night*
*sounds of summer*

*die Frösche in meinem Teich*
*krächzen in der warmen Nacht*
*sind die Klänge des Sommers*

*les grenouilles de mon étang*
*coassent dans la nuit chaude*
*ce sont les sons de l´été*

*las ranas de mi lago*
*croando en la noche cálida*
*son los sonidos del verano*

157.

pequeno ribeiro
que corria perto da vila –
cristal líquido

*little brook*
*that ran close to the village –*
*liquid crystal*

*kleines Bächlein*
*die in der Nähe des Dorfes verlief –*
*Flüssigkristal*

*petit ruisseau*
*qui coulait près du village –*
*cristal liquide*

*pequeño arroyo*
*que corría cerca de la aldea –*
*cristal líquido*

158.

ainda recordo
o sabor da água da fonte
onde, criança, bebia

[mais memórias da infância, das férias passadas em casa da avó paterna, bem no centro do país, numa aldeia onde havia um riacho de água cristalina e muitas fontes de água pura]

*I still remember*
*the taste of the spring water*
*where, a child, I drank*

*ich erinnere mich noch an*
*den Geschmack des Quellwassers*
*wo ich als Kind trank*

*je me souviens encore*
*du goût de l'eau de la fontaine*
*où, enfant, je buvais*

*todavia recuerdo*
*el sabor del agua de la fuente*
*dónde, niña, bebía*

* * *

71

159.

que estranho é
este súbito desejo
de viver em pleno

*how strange it is*
*this sudden desire*
*to live in full*

*wie seltsam es ist*
*dieser plötzliche Wunsch*
*voll und ganz zu leben*

*comme c´est étrange*
*ce désir soudain*
*de vivre pleinement*

*que extraño es*
*este súbito deseo*
*de vivir en pleno*

160.

melhor ou pior
cheguei a esta idade
agora o declínio...

*better or worse*
*I arrived at this age*
*now the decline...*

*besser oder schlechter*
*ich habe dieses Alter erreicht*
*jetzt der Absturz...*

*meilleur ou pire*
*je suis arrivée à cet âge*
*maintenant, le déclin...*

*mejor o peor*
*llegué a esta edad*
*ahora el declíneo...*

161.

o tempo passa
e nós mudamos com ele –
para sobreviver

*time goes by*
*and we change with it –*
*to survive*

*die Zeit vergeht*
*und wir haben uns damit verändert –*
*um zu überleben*

*le temps passe*
*et nous changeons avec lui –*
*pour survivre*

*el tiempo passa*
*y nosotros cambiamos com él –*
*para sobrevivir*

162.

eu sempre soube
que vinha aqui parar –
era o meu destino

*I´ve always known*
*that I would end up here –*
*it was my fate*

*ich wusste immer*
*dass ich hierher komme –*
*es war mein Schicksal*

*j´ai toujours su*
*que j´arriverai a ce point –*
*c´était mon destin*

*siempre supe*
*que llegaría  aqui –*
*era mi destino*

163.

se não dormisse...
teria tempo de ler
todos os meus livros?

*if I didn´t sleep...*
*would I have the time to read*
*all my books?*

*wenn ich nicht geschlafen habe...*
*ich hätte Zeit zum Lesen*
*alle meine Bücher?*

*si je ne dormais pas...*
*aurais-je le temps de lire*
*tous mes livres?*

*si no durmiera...*
*tendría tiempo de leer*
*todos mis libros?*

* * *

164.

porquê agora
nesta fase da vida, esta
sensação de harmonia?

*why now*
*at this point in life, this*
*feeling of harmony?*

*warum jetzt*
*in diesem Lebensabschnitt, dieses*
*Gefühl der Harmonie?*

*pourquoi maintenant*
*à ce stade de la vie, ce*
*sentiment d´harmonie?*

*por que ahora*
*en esta fase de la vida, esta*
*sensación de armonía?*

165.

tudo tem um fim
para que tudo continue
é a lei da vida

*everything has an end*
*so everything can go on*
*it´s the law of life*

*alles hat ein Ende*
*damit alles weitergehen kann*
*das ist das Lebensgesetz*

*tout a une fin*
*pour que tout continue*
*c´est la loi de la vie*

*todo tiene un final*
*para que todo continue*
*es la ley de la vida*

166.

a lua, frio e escuro
o sol, calor, luz, energia
ambos dão vida…

*the moon, cold and dark*
*the sun, heat, light, energy*
*both give life…*

*der Mond, kalt und dunkel*
*die Sonne, die Wärme, das Licht, die Energie*
*beide schenken das Leben…*

*la lune, froide et sombre*
*le soleil, chaleur, lumière, énergie*
*les deux donnent la vie…*

*la luna, frio y oscuro*
*el sol, calor, luz, energia*
*ambos dan la vida…*

\* \* \*

167.

se a chuva lavasse
os males deste mundo
oh! que bom este ano...

*if the rain could wash*
*the evils of this world*
*oh! how good would be this year...*

*wenn der Regen das Übel*
*wegspült dieser Welt*
*oh! wie gut dieses Jahr ist...*

*si la pluie lavait*
*les maux de ce monde*
*oh! comme cette année serait bonne...*

*si la lluvia lavara*
*los males de este mundo*
*oh! que bueno este año...*

168.

na mesa, o relógio
mostra como a nossa vida
se evapora...

*on the table, the clock*
*shows how our life*
*vanishes into thin air...*

*auf dem Tisch, die Uhr*
*zeigt wie unser Leben*
*es verdunstet...*

*sur la table, l'horloge*
*montre comme notre vie*
*s'évapore...*

*en la mesa, el reloj*
*nos enseña como*
*se evapora la vida...*

169.

neste nosso mundo
não há plano nem objetivo
cada um responsável...

*in this world of ours*
*there is no plan or objective*
*each one responsible...*

*in dieser unserer Welt*
*gibt es keinen Plan und kein Ziel*
*jeder einzelne ist verantwortlich...*

*dans notre monde*
*il n´y pas de plan ou d´objectif*
*chacun responsable...*

*en nuestro mundo*
*no hay plan ni objetivo*
*cada uno responsable...*

* * *

170.

ainda está frio
nas árvores os pássaros
tufam as penas

*still cold*
*on the trees the birds*
*tuft their feathers*

*es ist immer noch kalt*
*in den Bäumen die Vögel*
*ihr Gefieder büschelt*

*il fait encore froid*
*sur les arbres, les oiseaux*
*touffent les plumes*

*todavía está frío*
*en los árboles los pájaros*
*tufan las plumas*

171.

noite de lua nova
silêncio e escuridão
em sintonia

*new moon night*
*silence and darkness*
*in harmony*

*neue Mondnacht*
*Stille und Dunkelheit*
*in Synchroniserung*

*nuit de nouvelle lune*
*silence et obscurité*
*en harmonie*

*noche de luna nueva*
*silencio y oscuridad*
*en sintonía*

172.

flamingos brancos
pousam na água-espelho
logo duplicados

*white flamingos*
*they land on the mirror-water*
*at once duplicated*

*weiße Flamingos*
*auf dem Spiegelwasser landen*
*bald verviefältigt*

*flamants blancs*
*ils atterrissent sur l'eau-mirroir*
*soudain en doubles*

*flamencos blancos*
*posan en el agua-espejo*
*luego duplicados*

173.

um arrulhar ao longe
tantos outros trinados
sinfonia genial

*a cakle in the distance*
*so many other bird songs*
*great symphony*

*ein korken in der Ferne*
*so viele andere Vögel Singerei*
*große Symphonie*

*roucoulement au loin*
*tellement d´autres trilles*
*grande symphonie*

*un arrullar a lo lejos*
*tantos otros trinos*
*sinfonía genial*

* * *

174.

cabelos de prata
cobrem a minha cabeça
velha, não sábia...

*silver hair*
*covers my head*
*old, not wise...*

*silbernes Haar*
*bedecke meinen Kopf*
*alt, nicht weise...*

*cheveux d´argent*
*couvrent ma tête*
*vieille-femme, pas sage...*

*cabellos de plata*
*cubren mi cabeza*
*vieja, no sabia...*

175.

comer, ser comido
é a lei da vida
sempre cumprida…

*eat, be eaten*
*it is the law of life*
*always fulfilled…*

*essen, gegessen werden*
*ist das Gesetz des Lebens*
*stets erfüllt…*

*manger, être mangé*
*c´est la loi de la vie*
*toujours complète…*

*comer, ser comido*
*es la ley de la vida*
*siempre cumplida…*

\* \* \*

176.

aqui estou de novo
no pedaço de paraíso
imerecido

*here am I again*
*in my piece of paradise*
*undeserved*

*hier bin ich wieder*
*in dem Stück Paradies*
*unverdient*

*me voici à nouveau*
*dans le coin de paradis*
*non mérité*

*aqui estoy de nuevo*
*en el pedazo de paraíso*
*inmerecido*

177.

som de mar ao longe
nada mais – como se a terra
vazia estivesse...

*sound of the sea in the distance*
*nothing more – as if the earth*
*was empty...*

*Rauschen des Meeres in der Ferne*
*nichts mehr – als od die Erde*
*leer sei...*

*le bruit de la mer au loin*
*rien de plus – comme si la terre*
*était vide...*

*sonido de mar a lo lejos*
*nada más – como si la tierra*
*estuviera vacía...*

178.

tic, tac, tic, tac, tic...
os segundos escoam-se
líquido o tempo...

*tick, tock, tick, tock, tick...*
*the seconds flow away*
*like time was liquid...*

*tic, tac, tic, tac, tic...*
*die Sekunden fließen aus*
*flüssige Zeit...*

*tic, tac, tic, tac, tic...*
*les secondes s´écoulent*
*liquide est le temps...*

*tic, tac, tic, tac, tic...*
*los segundos se alejan*
*líquido el tiempo...*

179.

primeiros raios
os seres animados
despertam do sono

*first rays*
*the animate beings*
*wake up from sleep*

*erste Strahlen*
*die belebten Wesen*
*aus dem Schlaf erwachen*

*premiers rayons*
*les êtres animés*
*se réveillent de leur sommeil*

*primeiros rayos*
*los seres animados*
*despertan del sueño*

180.

fiquei a pensar –
quando os anjos dormem
quem vela por nós?

*I was thinking –*
*when the angels sleep*
*who watches over us?*

*das hat mich zum Nachdenken gebracht –*
*wenn die Engel schlafen*
*wer wacht über uns?*

*je pensais –*
*quand les anges dorment*
*qui nous surveille?*

*me quedé pensando –*
*quando los ángeles duermen*
*quién vela por nosotros?*

181.

ontem tão azul
hoje cinzento – o mar, do céu
reflexo escurecido

*yesterday so blue*
*gray today – the sea, from the sky*
*dark reflection*

*gestern so blau*
*heute grau – das Meer, der Himmel*
*ein verdunkeltes Spiegelbild*

*hier tellement bleue*
*aujourd´hui grise – la mer, du ciel*
*reflet sombre*

*ayer tan azul*
*hoy gris – el mar, del cielo*
*reflejo oscurecido*

182.

na trovoada
o raio fendeu o pinheiro
só metade morto

[no regresso da casa da Galé vi um pinheiro bravo grande fendido a meio, com
uma das metades verde e a outra metade seca, terá sido um raio que o atingiu]

*in a thunderstorm*
*the ray split the pine*
*only half dead*

*im Gewittersturm*
*der Blitz spaltete die Kiefer*
*nur halb tot*

*dans l'orage*
*l'éclair a divisé le pin*
*seulement à moitié mort*

*en la tormenta*
*rajó el pino*
*sólo la mitad muerto*

183.

chocando o[s] ovo[s]
a cegonha-mãe, no ninho
paciente, aguarda

*hatching the egg[s]*
*mother stork, in the nest*
*patiently, awaits*

*ausbrüten des Eies[s]*
*der Storchenmutter, im Nest*
*Patient, abwarten*

*couvant l´ [les] oeuf[s]*
*la mère cigogne, dans le nid*
*patiente, attend*

*incubando el [los] huevo[s]*
*la cigueña-madre, en el nido*
*paciente, espera*

\* \* \*

184.

uma coisa sei
eu não sou este corpo
mas vivo nele

*one thing I know*
*I am not this body*
*but I live in it*

*eines weiß ich*
*ich bin nicht dieser Körper*
*aber ich lebe in ihm*

*une chose que je sais*
*je ne suis pas ce corps*
*mais je vis dedans*

*una cosa sé*
*no soy este cuerpo*
*pero vivo en él*

185.

o nosso corpo
é sempre um mistério
que mal controlamos

*our body*
*is always a mistery*
*we barely control*

*unser Körper*
*ist immer ein Rätsel*
*den wir kaum kontrollieren können*

*notre corps*
*est toujours un mystère*
*que nous contrôlons à peine*

*nuestro cuerpo*
*es sempre un mistério*
*que mal controlamos*

186.

não devíamos ser
o centro do nosso mundo
nem o seu limite

*we shouldn't be*
*the center of our world*
*nor its limit*

*wir sollten nicht*
*das Zentrum unserer Welt sein*
*weder seine Grenze*

*nous ne devrions pas être*
*le centre de notre monde*
*ni sa limite non plus*

*no deberíamos ser*
*el centro de nuestro mundo*
*ni su limite*

* * *

187.

feliz, o cão corre
no jardim, atrás do dono
seu único deus

*joyfull, the dog runs*
*in the garden, behind his owner*
*his only god*

*glüklich, der Hund läuft*
*im Garten, nach seinem Herrn*
*sein einziger Gott*

*heureux, le chien court*
*dans le jardin, derrière son propriétaire*
*son seul dieu*

*feliz, el perro corre*
*en el jardín, detrás del dueño*
*su único dios*

188.

o gato, ser felino
caminha com elegância
seguro de si

*the cat, feline being*
*walks elegantly*
*sure of itself*

*die Katze, das katzenartige Wesen*
*geht mit Eleganz*
*selbstbewusst*

*le chat, être félin*
*marche élégamment*
*sûr de lui-même*

*el gato, ser felino*
*camina com elegancia*
*seguro de si*

\* \* \*

189.

como noite e dia
assim o mal e o bem
inevitáveis?

*like day and night*
*also good and evil*
*inevitable?*

*wie Tag und Nacht*
*folglich böse und gute*
*unvermeidlich?*

*comme nuit et jour*
*le mal et le bien aussi*
*inévitables?*

*como noche y día*
*así el bien y el mal*
*inevitables?*

190.

olho o passado
o que fiz de errado?
o que aprendi?

*I look back*
*what have I done wrong?*
*what did I learn?*

*ich schaue auf die Vergangenheit*
*was habe ich falsch gemacht?*
*was habe ich gelernt?*

*je regarde le passé*
*qu´est-ce que j´ai fait de mal?*
*qu´ai-je appris?*

*miro el passado*
*qué hice mal?*
*qué aprendí?*

\* \* \*

87

191.

a lua redonda
suspensa no céu escuro
suave nos toca

*the round moon*
*suspended in the dark sky*
*softly touches us*

*der runde Mond*
*im dunklen Himmel schwebend*
*berührt uns sanft*

*la lune ronde*
*suspendue dans le ciel sombre*
*doucement nous touche*

*la luna redonda*
*suspendida en el cielo oscuro*
*suave nos toca*

192.

luz na janela
um autocarro passa
mais um dia começa

*light in the window*
*a bus passes by*
*a new day begins*

*Licht im Fenster*
*ein Bus fährt vorbei*
*ein neuer Tag beginnt*

*lumière dans la fenêtre*
*un autocar passe*
*un autre jour commence*

*luz en la ventana*
*un autobus pasa*
*un día más empieza*

193.

descer a rua
bebericando café –
como num filme!

going down the street
slowly drinking coffee –
like in a movie!

die Straße hinuntergehen
Kaffee zu genießen –
wie in einem film!

marcher dans la rue
en buvant un café –
comme dans un film!

descender la calle
bebiendo café –
como en una película!

194.

o amolador passou
entoando o seu apito –
amanhã chove

the cutler passed by
playing his whistle –
tomorrow it rains

die Scherenschleifer ging vorbei
setzen sie ihre Pfeiffer auf –
Morgen regnet es

l'affûteur est passé
en sifflotant –
demain il pleut

el afilador de tijeras pasó
tocando su silbata –
mañana llueve

195.

bom cheiro a relva
acabada de cortar
frescura verde

*good smell of*
*freshly cut grass*
*green freshness*

*guter Geruch nach Gras*
*frischer schnitt*
*grüne Frische*

*bonne odeur de l´herbe*
*qui vient d´être coupée*
*fraîcheur verte*

*buen olor a hierba*
*acabada de cortar*
*frescura verde*

196.

silvo de andorinha
rasgando o céu azul –
voava contigo...

*swallow hiss*
*ripping the blue sky –*
*I would fly with you...*

*Schwalbenrauschen*
*die den blauen Himmel zerreißen –*
*ich würde mit dir fliegen...*

*sifflement de l'hirondelle*
*déchirant le ciel bleu –*
*je volerais avec toi...*

*silbido de golondrina*
*rasgando el cielo azul –*
*volaria contigo...*

A partir de abril de 2018

197.

minhoca no bico
a ave pousou na árvore –
vida e morte

worm in the beak
the bird landed on the tree –
life and death

Wurm im Schnabel
der Vogel landete auf dem Baum –
Leben und Tod

un vers dans le bec
l'oiseau s'est posé sur l'arbre –
la vie et la mort

gusano en el pico
el ave se posó en el árbol –
vida y muerte

198.

ao vento forte
o espantalho parece
dizer-nos adeus

in the strong wind
the scarecrow seems
to wave us goodbye

im starken Wind
die Vogelscheuche scheint
verabschieden sie sich von uns

dans le vent fort
l'épouvantail semble
nous dire au revoir

en el viento fuerte
el espantapájaros parece
decirnos adiós

\*\*\*

199.

que me aconteceu
entre duas estações de metro –
lapso no tempo?

[entre duas estações do metro tive a sensação de me ter "ausentado" –
adormecido? durante uns instantes?...]

*what happened to me*
*in-between two subway stations –*
*a lapse in time?*

*was mir passiert ist*
*zwischen zwei U-Bahn Stationen –*
*die Zeit vergeht?*

*ce qui m'est arrivé*
*entre deux stations de métro –*
*une pause dans le temps?*

*que me sucedió*
*entre dos estaciones de metro –*
*lapso en el tiempo?*

\*\*\*

200.

na borda do lago
o pato, escondido
arruma as penas

*on the brim of the lake*
*hidden, the duck*
*combs its feathers*

*am Rande des Sees*
*die Ente, versteckt*
*räumt sein Gefieder auf*

*au bord du lac*
*le canard, caché*
*arrange ses plumes*

*al borde del lago*
*el pato escondido*
*arregla las plumas*

201.

mãe pata, atenta
vigia a nova ninhada
tão irrequieta

*mother goose, attentive*
*watches the new litter*
*so restless*

*Entenmutter, wachsam*
*beobachtet die neue Brut*
*so unruhig*

*mère canard, attentive*
*regarde la nouvelle portée*
*tellement agitée*

*madre pata, atenta*
*vigila sus nuevas crias*
*tan inquietas*

202.

o cheiro a terra
acorda velhas memórias
de tempos mais simples

*the smell of revolved earth*
*awakens old memories*
*of simpler times*

*der Geruch der Erde*
*weckt alte Erinnerungen*
*aus einfacheren Zeiten*

*l'odeur de terre labourée*
*réveille de vieux souvenirs*
*des temps plus simples*

*el olor de la tierra revuelta*
*despierta viejos recuerdos*
*de tiempos más simples*

203.

entre as folhas secas
o rouxinol saltita –
que procura ele?

*on the dry leaves*
*the nightingale is leaping –*
*what is it looking for?*

*inmittten der trockenen Blättern*
*springt die Nachtigall –*
*wonach suchst sie?*

*entre les feuilles sèches*
*le rossignol saute –*
*que cherches-tu?*

*entre las hojas secas*
*el ruiseñor salta –*
*qué busca?*

204.

a rã, plácida
sobre o nenúfar, aguarda
que a mosca passe

*the frog, placidly*
*on the water lily, awaits*
*the fly to pass*

*der Frosch, friedlich*
*auf der Seerose, wartet auf*
*die vorbeifliegende Fliege*

*la grenouille, placide*
*sur le nénuphar, attend*
*passer la mouche*

*la rana, plácida*
*sobre el nenúfar, aguarda*
*que la mosca passe*

205.

que bom odor é este
que a brisa traz ao nariz?
primavera mix!

*what sweet odor is this*
*that the breeze brings to my nose?*
*springtime mix!*

*was ist das für ein guter Geruch*
*die die Brise zur Nase führt?*
*Frühlingsmischung!*

*quelle bonne odeur est-ce*
*que la brise apporte à mon nez?*
*mélange de printemps!*

*que buen olor es este*
*que la brisa trae a la nariz?*
*mezcla de primavera!*

\*\*\*

206.

o pouco que sei
da vida das criaturas
muito me fascina

*the little that I know*
*of creatures' lives*
*really fascinates me*

*das Wenige, das ich weiß*
*über das Leben der Geschöpfe*
*fasziniert mich sehr*

*le peu que je connaisse*
*de la vie des créatures*
*me fascine profondément*

*lo poco que sé*
*de la vida de las criaturas*
*cuánto me fascina*

207.

voa presa ao fio
borboleta de papel –
é o meu retrato...

[vi no centro comercial uma borboleta de papel que voava presa a um fio, e
pensei na minha vida, presa à diálise...]

*flies hung by a wire*
*paper butterffly –*
*it's my portrait...*

*fliegt die beute auf den Draht*
*Papierschmetterling –*
*ist mein Porträt...*

*vole attaché au fil*
*papillon en papier –*
*c'est mon portrait...*

*vuela amarrada al hilo*
*mariposa de papel –*
*es mi retrato...*

\*\*\*

208.

nuvem amarela –
todos os pinheiros soltam pólen
no mesmo instante

[uma única vez assisti na primavera, da janela da casa da Galé, a este
momento mágico da polinização dos pinheiros exatamente ao mesmo tempo!]

*yellow cloud –*
*all the pine trees release pollen*
*at the exact same time*

*gelbe Wolke –*
*alle Nadelbäume setzen Pollen frei*
*zur gleichen Zeit*

*nuage jaune –*
*tous les pins libèrent du pollen*
*en même temps*

*nube amarilla –*
*todos los pinos sueltan polen*
*en el mismo instante*

\*\*\*

209.

somos como pássaros
presos nas suas gaiolas
sonhando ser livres

*we are like birds*
*trapped in their cages*
*dreaming of being free*

*wir sind wie Vögel*
*in ihren Käfigen gefangen*
*träumen davon frei zu sein*

*nous sommes comme des oiseaux*
*pris au piège dans leurs cages*
*rêvant d'être libres*

*somos como pájaros*
*presos en sus jaulas*
*soñando ser libres*

210.

a natureza
não é feliz nem moral –
nós somos seus filhos...

*nature*
*is neither happy nor moral –*
*we are her children...*

*die Natur*
*ist weder glücklich noch moralisch –*
*wir sind deine Kinder...*

*la nature*
*n´est ni heureuse ni morale –*
*nous sommes ses enfants...*

*la naturaleza*
*no es feliz ni moral –*
*nosotros somos sus hijos...*

211.

que pássaro canta
à primeira luz da manhã?
velho companheiro...

[nas minhas noites perdidas, às primeiras horas da madrugada, ouço sempre o canto dum pássaro que não sei identificar, momentos antes do meu mandarim na gaiola na cozinha]

*what bird sings*
*at the first light of dawn?*
*old friend...*

*welcher Vogel singt*
*beim ersten Morgenlicht?*
*alter Freund...*

*quel oiseau chante*
*à la première heure du matin?*
*vieil ami...*

*que pájaro canta*
*a la primera luz de la mañana?*
*viejo compañero...*

\*\*\*

212.

som cavo ao longe –
cegonhas batendo bicos
no alto da torre

*hollow sound in the distance –*
*storks beating beaks*
*on the top of the tower*

*hohles Geräusch in der Ferne –*
*Störche, klappern mit dem Schnabel*
*auf der Spitze des Turms*

*son sourd au loin –*
*cigognes battant du bec*
*au sommet de la tour*

*un sonido sordo a lo lejos –*
*cigüeñas golpean con sus picos*
*en lo alto de la torre*

213.

perfeito movimento –
a águia desliza no céu
suspensa na brisa

*perfect movement –*
*the eagle glides in the sky*
*suspended in the breeze*

*perfekter Bewegung –*
*der Adler gleitet in den Himmel*
*in der Brise aufgehängt*

*mouvement parfait –*
*l'aigle glisse dans le ciel*
*suspendu dans la brise*

*perfecto movimiento –*
*el águila se desliza en el cielo*
*suspendida en la brisa*

\*\*\*

214.

quando eu morrer
as mágoas que ficam –
quem deixo atrás...

*when I die*
*the sorrows that remain –*
*the ones I leave behind...*

*wenn ich sterbe*
*die Sorgen, die bleiben –*
*die ich zurücklasse...*

*quand je vais mourir*
*les chagrins qui restent –*
*ceux que je laisse derrière...*

*cuando yo me muera*
*las penas que se quedan –*
*quién dejo atrás...*

215.

como num instante
tudo muda! – nada somos,
nada valemos

[este e o seguinte foram compostos depois de um dia em que tive problemas
com a fístula e pensei que teria de em breve ir ao hospital para me fazerem
outra]

*how in an instant*
*everything changes! – we are nothing,*
*we are valueless*

*wie in einem Augenblick*
*ändert sich alles! – wir sind nichts*
*wir sind wertlos*

*comme en un instant*
*tout change! – nous ne sommes rien,*
*nous ne valons rien*

*como en un instante*
*¡todo cambia! – no somos nada,*
*nada valemos*

100

216.

milagres não há
mas eu bem precisava
de um agora...

*there are no miracles*
*but I really needed one*
*right now...*

*es gibt keine Wunder*
*aber ich könnte wirklich eins brauchen*
*aber sofort...*

*miracles il n'y en a pas*
*mais j'en avais vraiment besoin*
*d'un maintenant...*

*milagros no los hay*
*pero yo necesito realmente*
*uno ahora...*

***

217.

na manhã fresca
o café conforta o corpo
e aquece a alma

*in the cold morning*
*a cup of coffee comforts the body*
*and warms the soul*

*am kühlen Morgen*
*Kaffee tröstet den Körper*
*und wärmt die Seele*

*un matin frais*
*un café réconforte le corps*
*et réchauffe l'âme*

*en la mañana fresca*
*el café conforta el cuerpo*
*y calienta el alma*

218.

noite já tarde
o corpo pede descanso
a mente não para...

*late night*
*the body demands for rest*
*the mind keeps running...*

*spät in der Nacht*
*der Körper verlangt nach Ruhe*
*der Verstand bleibt nicht stehen...*

*tard dans la nuit*
*le corps demande du repos*
*l'esprit ne s'arrête pas...*

*noche ya tarde*
*el cuerpo pide descanso*
*la mente no para...*


219.

noite agitada.
que inundação de luz e sons
ao raiar do dia

*hectic night.*
*what flood of light and sounds*
*at daybreak*

*unruhige Nacht*
*was für eine Flut von Licht und Klang*
*bei Tagesanbruch*

*nuit agitée.*
*inondation de lumière et de sons*
*au lever du jour*

*noche inquieta.*
*que inundación de luz y sonidos*
*al rayar del día*

220.

o verão não chega
dias cinzentos e feios
saudades do sol...

*summer is late*
*gray ugly days*
*I miss the sun...*

*der Sommer kommt nicht*
*graue und hässliche Tage*
*Sehnsucht nach der Sonne...*

*l'été n'arrive pas*
*jours gris et laids*
*le soleil me manque...*

*el verano no llega*
*días grises y feos*
*añelo el sol...*

221.

apesar da chuva
a planície a ficar amarela
cumpre-se o ciclo

*despite the rain*
*the plain is turning yellow*
*the cycle is fulfilled*

*trotz des Regens*
*die Ebene wird gelb*
*der Zyklus ist erfüllt*

*malgré la pluie*
*la plaine devient jaune*
*le cycle est accompli*

*a pesar de la lluvia*
*la planicie se vuelve amarilla*
*se cumple el ciclo*

[escrito, e os dois seguintes, num regresso a Lisboa depois de mais um fim de
semana no Alentejo em junho 2018]

222.

lindo tapete
verde, ainda cobre os campos –
parece veludo

*beautiful green*
*rug, still covers the fields –*
*it looks like velvet*

*schön grün*
*bedeckt noch die Felder –*
*sieht aus wie Samt*

*beau tapis*
*vert, couvre encore les champs –*
*on dirait du velours*

*hermosa alfombra*
*verde, aún cubre los campos –*
*parece terciopelo*

223.

troncos vermelhos –
nova leva de sobreiros
a dar cortiça

*reddish tree trunks –*
*new batch of cork oaks*
*giving cork*

*rote Stämme –*
*neue Partie Korkeichen geben*
*schenkende Korken*

*les troncs rouges –*
*nouvelle couche d'écorce*
*donnant du liège*

*troncos rojos –*
*nueva toma de alcornoques*
*dando corcho*

\*\*\*

224.

cabelo ao vento
céu azul, sol morno – quase
me senti livre...

*hair in the wind*
*blue sky, warm sun – I almost*
*felt free...*

*Haare im Wind*
*blauer Himmel, warme Sonne - fast*
*ich fühlte mich frei...*

*cheveux au vent*
*ciel bleu, soleil chaud - je me sentais*
*presque libre...*

*cabellos al viento*
*cielo azul, sol tibio - casi*
*me sentí libre...*

225.

a vida não para
e eu a correr atrás dela
sem a apanhar

*life does not stop*
*and me running after it*
*without catching it*

*das Leben bleibt nicht stehen*
*und ich renne hinter dem Leben her*
*ohne es zu fassen*

*la vie ne s'arrête pas*
*et moi courant après elle*
*sans l'attraper*

*la vida no para*
*y yo corriendo detrás de ella*
*sin recogerla*

\*\*\*

226.

ouvindo música
deslizando pela estrada –
momento perfeito

*listening to music*
*sliding down the road –*
*perfect moment*

*Musik hören*
*die Straße entlangzugleiten –*
*perfekter moment*

*écoutant de la musique*
*glissant sur la route –*
*moment parfait*

*escuchando música*
*deslizando por la carretera –*
*tiempo perfecto*

\*\*\*

227.

ao longe o mar
sussurra nas ondas
a melodia eterna

*in the distance the sea*
*whispers in the waves*
*the eternal melody*

*In der Ferne das Meer*
*geflüster in den Wellen*
*die ewige Melodie*

*au loin la mer*
*murmure dans les vagues*
*la mélodie éternelle*

*a lo lejos el mar*
*susurra en las olas*
*la melodía eterna*

228.

penas coloridas
esvoaçam junto ao lago
fonte de vida

colourful feathers
flutter near the pond
source of life

bunte Federn
Flattern am See
Quelle des Lebens

plumes colorées
volent près du lac
source de vie

plumas de colores
revoluteando junto al lago
fuente de vida

229.

na tarde quente
o abelhão para na flor
sugando nectar

in the warm afternoon
the bee stopped on the flower
sucking nectar

an einem heißen Nachmittag
die Hummel bleibt an der Blume stehen
um Blütennektar zu saugen

dans l'après-midi chaud
l'abeille s´arrête sur une fleur
pour sucer le nectar

en la tarde caliente
la abeja para sobre la flor
sorviendo el néctar

***

230.

na noite morna
um zumbido irritante
quebra o bom sono

*in the warm night*
*an annoying buzzing sound*
*breaks my sleep*

*in der warmen Nacht*
*ein irritierendes Brummen*
*unterbricht den guten Schlaf*

*dans la nuit chaude*
*un bourdonnement agaçant*
*brise le bon sommeil*

*en la noche caliente*
*un zumbido irritante*
*rompe el buen sueño*

231.

que saudades
de noite inteira de sono
como em criança!

*how I miss*
*a whole night's sleep*
*like when I was a child!*

*wie sehr ich es vermisse*
*eine ganze Nacht zu schlafen*
*wie ein Kind!*

*tu me manques*
*nuit tranquile de sommeil*
*comme dort un enfant!*

*qué nostalgia*
*de una noche entera de sueño*
*como la infancia!*

232.

vejo estrelas
da janela do quarto –
eu nasci delas

I see the stars
from my bedroom window –
I come from them

ich sehe Sterne
aus dem Schlafzimmerfenster –
ich wurde von ihnen geboren

je vois des étoiles
de la fenêtre de ma chambre –
je suis née d'elles

veo estrellas
de la ventana de la habitación –
yo nací de ellas

233.

já fui poeira
no caos primordial –
pó serei de novo

dust I was
in the primordial caos –
dust I shall be again

ich war einst Staub
im Ur-Chaos –
Staub werde ich wieder sein

j'étais poussière
dans le chaos primordial –
poussière je serai à nouveau

ya he sido polvo
en el caos primordial –
polvo seré de nuevo

\*\*\*

109

234.

no céu de verão
a cegonha desliza
por puro prazer

[no regresso do Alentejo vi uma cegonha voar muito alto, em círculos, não parecia andar à procura de comida, apenas a apreciar o vôo...]

in the summer sky
the white stork glides
just for sheer delight

unter dem Sommerhimmel
der Storch gleitet
zum reinen Vergnügen

dans le ciel d'été
la cigogne glisse
par pur plaisir

en el cielo de verano
la cigüeña se desliza
por puro plácer

235.

num dia tão bonito
apetece ir pelo caminho
longo para casa...

[escrito num regresso a casa a ouvir Supertramp... claro]

on such a lovely day
feels like taking
the long way home...

ich habe Lust,
den langen Weg zu nehmen
der lange Weg nach hause...

dans cette si belle journée
je veux aller par le chemin
le plus long à la maison...

en un día tan hermoso
me siento como tomar el camino
largo a casa...

236.

o verão é bom –
dias longos, sol, calor
a vida mais leve...

*summer is good –*
*long days, sunny skies, warm breeze*
*life feels lighter...*

*der Sommer ist gut –*
*lange Tage, Sonne, Hitze*
*das leichtere Leben...*

*l'été c'est bien –*
*longues journées, soleil, chaleur*
*la vie plus légère...*

*el verano es bueno –*
*días largos, sol, calor*
*la vida más ligera...*

\*\*\*

237.

seus olhos lânguidos
povoaram meus sonhos –
estranho encanto...

[uma noite em que tive um sono agitado acordei com este pequeno poema na
cabeça, sem perceber de onde veio – algum sonho que tive? Alguma relação
com um documentário que vi recentemente na TV sobre o Japão?]

*his languid eyes*
*filled my dreams –*
*strange charm...*

*deine trüben Augen*
*erfüllten meine Träume –*
*seltsame Verzauberung...*

*ses yeux languissants*
*ont peuplé mes rêves –*
*étrange charme...*

*sus ojos lánguidos*
*poblaran mis sueños –*
*extraño encanto...*

238.

primeira luz –
sem sono, apetece a hora
do dia começar

*first morning light –*
*not sleepy, I wish for the time*
*to start my day*

*erstes Licht –*
*ohne schlaf, ist es Zeit*
*für den Beginn des Tages*

*première lumière –*
*sans sommeil, j´ai envie*
*de commencer ma journée*

*primera luz –*
*sin sueño, añora la hora*
*en que empieza el día*

239.

a vida agora
tem sempre este ritmo:
o dia sim dia não…

*my life now*
*has forever  this new rythm:*
*every other day…*

*Leben nun*
*hat immer diesen Rhythmus:*
*tagein, tagaus…*

*la vie maintenant*
*a toujours ce rythme:*
*un jour oui, un jour non…*

*la vida ahora*
*siempre tiene este ritmo:*
*el día sí día no…*

\*\*\*

240.

verão, inverno
madrugada, os pássaros
o novo dia saúdam

summer, winter
at dawn, the birds
 greet the new day

Sommer, Winter
Morgengrauen, die Vögel
den neuen Tag begrüßen

été, hiver
l'aube, les oiseaux
le nouveau jour saluent

invierno, verano
madrugada, los pájaros
el nuevo día saludan

241.

o ar da manhã
é fresco e leve, tão diferente
do resto do dia

the morning air
it´s cool and light, so different
from the rest of the day

die Morgenluft
ist frisch und leicht, so anders
vom Rest des Tages

l'air du matin
est frais et léger, si différent
du reste de la journée

el aire de la mañana
es fresco y ligero, tan diferente
del resto del día

242.

natureza em flor
suaves odores no ar –
é pleno verão!

*blooming nature*
*sweet scents in the air –*
*it is midsummer!*

*blühende Natur*
*milde Gerüche in der Luft –*
*es ist Mittsommer!*

*nature en fleur*
*odeurs douces dans l'air –*
*c'est le milieu de l'été!*

*naturaleza en flor*
*suaves olores en el aire –*
*¡es pleno verano!*

243.

a meio do verão
já o alentejo a ficar
da cor da palha

*mid summer*
*already the alentejo turning*
*the color of straw*

*Mitten im Sommer*
*bereits der alentejo wird*
*die Farbe des Strohs*

*mi-été*
*déjà alentejo devient*
*couleur de paille*

*en medio del verano*
*ya alentejo quedandose*
*del color de la paja*

244.

efémera beleza –
seca, a rosa exala ainda
suave perfume

*ephemeral beauty –*
*dry, the rose still exhales*
*a soft perfume*

*flüchtige Schönheit –*
*getrocken, strahlt die Rose immer noch nach*
*zartes Parfüm*

*beauté éphémère –*
*sèche, la rose exhale encore*
*un doux parfum*

*efímera belleza –*
*seca, la rosa exhala todavía*
*suave perfume*

245.

céu azul de verão
tantos cantos de pássaros
se ouvem no ar!

*summer blue sky*
*so many bird songs*
*can be heard in the air!*

*blauer Sommerhimmel*
*so viele Vogelgesänge*
*kann man in der Luft hören!*

*ciel bleu d'été*
*tant de chants d'oiseaux*
*on entend dans l'air!*

*cielo azul de verano*
*tantos cantos de pájaros*
*¡se oyen en el aire!*

246.

troncos vermelhos –
a cada nove anos
ciclo de cortiça

*red trunks –*
*every nine years*
*cork cycle*

*rote Stämme –*
*alle neun Jahre*
*Korkenzyklus*

*troncs rouges –*
*tous les neuf ans*
*cycle du liège*

*troncos rojos –*
*cada nueve años*
*el ciclo del corcho*

247.

na tarde quente
a cegonha altiva
pousa num ramo

*in the hot afternoon*
*the haughty stork*
*lands on a branch*

*an einem warmen Nachmittag*
*der stolze Storch*
*sitzt auf einem Ast*

*dans l'après-midi chaud*
*la cigogne hautaine*
*atterrit sur une branche*

*en la tarde caliente*
*la cigüeña altiva*
*se pone en una rama*

248.

vila deserta –
no alentejo profundo
o calor aperta

*deserted village –*
*in the deep alentejo*
*the heat burns*

*verlassenes Dorf –*
*im tiefen alentejo*
*die Hitze spannt sich an*

*village abandonné –*
*dans le profond alentejo*
*la chaleur brûle*

*pueblo desierto –*
*alentejo profundo*
*el calor quema*

249.

outra insónia
logo aos primeiros raios
chilreia a passarada

*another sleepless night*
*at the first rays of day*
*so many birds chirp*

*eine weitere Schlaflosigkeit*
*bei den ersten Strahlen*
*die Vögel zwitschern*

*autre insomnie*
*aux premiers rayons*
*tant d'oiseaux gazouillent*

*otro insomnio*
*a los primeros rayos*
*chillan tantos pájaros*

250.

tanta chilreada
ensurdece o insone
já desesperado

*so much chirping*
*deafens someone*
*already desperate*

*so viel Gezwitscher*
*macht den Schlaflosen taub*
*bereits verzweifelt*

*tant de gazouillis*
*assourdissent quelqu'un*
*déjà désespéré*

*tanto chirrido*
*ensordece el insomne*
*ya desesperado*

251.

são três vezes três
as badaladas do sino
às seis da matina

*it's three times three*
*the bells of the belltower*
*at six o'clock in the morning*

*es ist drei mal drei*
*das Läunten der Glocke*
*um sechs Uhr morgens*

*ce sont trois fois trois*
*le carillon de la cloche*
*à six heures du matin*

*son tres veces tres*
*las campanadas del campanario*
*a las seis de la matina*

252.
    sol, águas calmas
    apetece mergulhar
    na albufeira

    *sun, calm waters*
    *I fancy diving*
    *in the reservoir*

    *Sonne, ruhige Gewässer*
    *Lust zum Tauchen*
    *im Reservoir*

    *soleil, eaux calmes*
    *j'ai envie de plonger*
    *dans le réservoir*

    *sol, aguas tranquilas*
    *me apetece bucear*
    *en la presa*

253.
    campos de arroz
    reflexos de água
    verde intenso

    *rice fields*
    *water reflections*
    *intense green*

    *Reisfelder*
    *Spiegelungen im wasser*
    *intensives Grün*

    *champs de riz*
    *reflets d'eau*
    *vert intense*

    *campos de arroz*
    *reflejos de agua*
    *verde intenso*

254.

a roda da vida
gira sem parar – e nós
morrendo aos poucos

*the wheel of life*
*keeps turning – and us*
*slowly dying*

*das Rad des Lebens*
*drecht sich endlos – und wir*
*sterben nach und nach*

*la roue de la vie*
*tourne sans s'arrêter – et nous*
*mourant lentement*

*la rueda de la vida*
*gira sin parar – y nosotros*
*muriendo poco a poco*

255.

calor finalmente!
é difícil respirar –
verão em pleno

*heat finally!*
*it's hard to breathe –*
*summer in full*

*endlich Hitze!*
*es ist schwer zu atmen –*
*Sommer in vollem Gange*

*chaleur enfin!*
*c'est dur de respirer –*
*plein été*

*calor por fin!*
*difícil respirar –*
*verano en pleno*

120

256.

começo os meus dias
sempre as mesmas voltas –
gosto da rotina

*I start my days*
*always the same rounds –*
*I enjoy the routine*

*ich beginne meine Tage*
*immer mit den gleichen Runden –*
*ich mag die Routine*

*je commence mes jours*
*toujours les mêmes courses –*
*j'aime la routine*

*comienzo mis días*
*siempre las mismas vueltas –*
*me gusta la rutina*

\*\*\*

257.

neblina no rio
calor sufocante
verão inclemente

*fog on the river*
*sweltering heat*
*inclement summer*

*Nebel im Fluss*
*brütende Hitze*
*rauer Sommer*

*brouillard sur la rivière*
*chaleur étouffante*
*été inclément*

*neblina en el río*
*calor sofocante*
*verano inclemente*

258.

florestas submersas:
tanta beleza no silêncio,
cheias de vida!

[em agosto no Oceanário de Lisboa vimos uma exposição de um japonês que
criou uns cenários de florestas submersas lindíssimas, cheias de plantas e
animais exóticos]

*submerged forests:*
*so much beauty in silence,*
*full of life!*

*überschwemmte Wälder:*
*so viel Schönheit in der Stille,*
*voller Leben!*

*forêts submergées:*
*tellement de beauté en silence,*
*pleines de vie!*

*bosques sumergidos:*
*cuanta belleza en el silencio,*
*llenos de vida!*

259.

de dia as cigarras,
na noite fresca os grilos –
são sons de verão!

*by day the cicadas,*
*in the cool night the crickets –*
*these are summer sounds!*

*tagsüber die Zikaden,*
*in der kühlen Nacht die Grillen –*
*sind die Klänge des Sommers!*

*de jour les cigales,*
*dans la nuit fraîche les grillons –*
*ce sont des sons d'été!*

*de día las cigarras,*
*en la noche fresca los grillos –*
*son sonidos de verano!*

260.

o vento varreu
as primeiras folhas secas –
verão a acabar

*the wind has blown
the first dry leaves –
summer is ending*

*der Wind verweht
die ersten trockenen Blätter –
der Sommer geht zu Ende*

*le vent a balayé
les premières feuilles séchées –
l'été s´en va*

*el viento barrió
las primeras hojas secas –
el verano se acaba*

\*\*\*

261.

estranho prazer
este, de beber café
amargo e quente...

*strange pleasure
this one, of drinking coffee
bitter and hot...*

*seltsames Vergnügen
dies, das Kaffeetrinken
bitter und heiß...*

*plaisir étrange
ceci, de boire du café
amer et chaud...*

*extraño placer este
de beber café
amargo y caliente...*

262.

a noite perdida
a sonhar que sou capaz
de criar algo belo...

*another lost night*
*dreaming of being able*
*to create something beautiful...*

*die verlorene Nacht*
*zu träumen, dass ich fähig bin*
*etwas Schönes zu erschaffen...*

*la nuit perdue*
*rêvant que je suis capable*
*de créer quelque chose de beau...*

*la noche perdida*
*a soñar que soy capaz*
*de crear algo hermoso...*

\*\*\*

263.

as folhas caídas
fazem um tapete fofo –
outono de novo

*the fallen leaves*
*make a soft rug –*
*autumn again*

*die abgefallenen Blätter*
*einen Flauschteppich legen –*
*Der Herbst ist wiedergekommen*

*les feuilles tombées*
*font un joli tapis –*
*l'automne de nouveau*

*las hojas caídas*
*hacen una alfombra mullida –*
*otoño de nuevo*

264.

o suave e ocre odor
das folhas secas no chão –
outono em pleno

*the soft ocher odor*
*of dried leaves on the floor –*
*autumn in full*

*der weiche, Okergeruch*
*von trockenen Blättern auf dem Boden –*
*Herbst in vollen Zügen*

*la douce odeur d'ocre*
*des feuilles séchées sur le sol –*
*automne en entier*

*el suave y ocre olor*
*de las hojas secas en el suelo –*
*otoño en pleno*

265.

belos tons de ocre
tingem a paisagem –
vida a apagar-se...

*beautiful shades of ocher*
*dye the landscape –*
*life is fading...*

*schöne Ockertöne*
*die Landschaft färben –*
*das Leben vergeht...*

*belles nuances d'ocre*
*teignent le paysage –*
*la vie s'éteint...*

*hermosos tonos de ocre*
*han teñido el paisaje –*
*vida que se apaga...*

\*\*\*

266.

a lua espreita
pelas frinchas da janela –
vê dentro de mim...

*the moon lurks*
*through the frills of the window –*
*looks inside me...*

*der Mond guckt heraus*
*durch die Lücken des Fensters –*
*sieht in mich hinein...*

*la lune se montre*
*par les fissures de la fenêtre –*
*et voit en moi...*

*la luna acecha*
*por las grietas de la ventana –*
*me ve por dentro...*

267.

mistério da vida –
porquê interessa a uns
e a outros nada?

*mystery of life –*
*why some are interested*
*and to others nothing?*

*Geheimnis des Lebens –*
*warum es für einige wichtig ist*
*und andere nicht?*

*mystère de la vie –*
*pourquoi certains sont intéressés*
*et d'autres rien?*

*el misterio de la vida –*
*por qué interesa a unos*
*y a otros nada?*

268.
na ânsia de viver
será que me esqueci
de dar amor aos outros?

in the eagerness to live
did I forget
to give love to others?

im Eifer des leben
habe ich vergessen
um anderen Liebe zu schenken?

dans le désir de vivre
est-ce que j'ai oublié
de donner de l'amour aux autres?

en el anhelo de vivir
es que me olvidé
de dar amor a los demás?

269.
as horas passam
eu de novo sem dormir
a pensar na vida...

the hours pass
me again not sleeping
thinking  about life...

die Stunden vergehen
wieder mich ohne Schlaf
über das Leben nachzudenken...

les heures passent
moi encore sans dormir
pensant à la vie...

las horas pasan
yo de nuevo sin dormir
pensando en la vida...

\*\*\*

270.

às seis da manhã
começa o movimento
o mundo acorda...

*at six in the morning*
*the movement begins*
*the world wakes up...*

*um sechs Uhr morgens*
*die Bewegung beginnt*
*die Welt wacht auf...*

*à six heures du matin*
*le mouvement commence*
*le monde se réveille...*

*a las seis de la mañana*
*comienza el movimiento*
*el mundo despierta...*

271.

o odor dos pinheiros
acorda belas memórias –
infância feliz...

*the odor of pine trees*
*wakes up beautiful memories –*
*happy childhood...*

*der Duft von Tannebäume*
*weckt schöne Erinnerungen –*
*glückliche Kindheit...*

*l'odeur des pins*
*réveille de beaux souvenirs –*
*enfance heureuse...*

*el olor de los pinos*
*despierta bellas memorias –*
*infancia feliz...*

272.

como fica bonito
depois das primeiras chuvas –
alentejo verde

*how beautiful it looks*
*after the first rains –*
*green alentejo*

*wie schön es aussieht*
*nach dem ersten Regen –*
*Grüner alentejo*

*comme c'est beau*
*après les premières pluies –*
*alentejo vert*

*como se pone bello*
*después de las primeras lluvias –*
*alentejo verde*

2019

273.

esta manhã vi
no caminho dos patos
o banho do melro

*this morning I saw*
*on the way of the ducks*
*the blackbird´s bath*

*heute morgen habe ich gesehen*
*auf dem Weg der Enten*
*das Amselbad*

*ce matin j'ai vu*
*sur le chemin des canards*
*le bain du merle*

*esta mañana he visto*
*en el camino de los patos*
*el baño del mirlo*

274.

no fundo do lago
as folhas secas de outono
tornaram-se brancas

*on the bottom of the lake*
*the dry autumn leaves*
*became white*

*auf dem Grund des Sees*
*das trockene Herbstlaub*
*ist weiß geworden*

*au fond du lac*
*les feuilles d'automne sèches*
*sont devenues blanches*

*en el fondo del lago*
*las hojas secas de otoño*
*se han vuelto blancas*

\*\*\*

275.

triste é perceber
que nem progresso nem saber
salvam este mundo...

*sad to realize*
*that neither progress nor knowledge*
*save this world...*

*traurig ist es zu erkennen*
*dass weder Fortschritt noch Erkenntnis*
*rette diese Welt...*

*triste de réaliser*
*que ni progrès ni connaissance*
*ne sauvent ce monde...*

*triste es percibir*
*que ni progreso ni saber*
*salvan este mundo...*

276.

ainda o inverno
mal começou e já sonho
com o sol de verão

*still winter*
*has just started and I already dream*
*of the summer sun*

*der winter ist noch da*
*hat kaum begonnen und schon träume ich*
*mit der Sommersonne*

*l'hiver encore*
*vient de commencer et je rêve déjà*
*au soleil d'été*

*todavía el invierno*
*mal comenzó y ya sueño*
*con el sol de verano*

277.

todos os dias
vou ver os patos nos lagos –
passeio de velhos...

*every day*
*I'm going to see the ducks in the ponds –*
*old folks´ stroll...*

*jeden Tag*
*werde ich die Enten auf den See betrachten –*
*Spaziergang der alten Leute...*

*tous les jours*
*je vais voir les canards dans les lacs –*
*promenade des vieillards...*

*todos los días*
*yo me voy a ver los patos en los lagos –*
*paseo de viejos ...*

278.

a noite tão fria
céu estrelado sem lua
e nada de sono...

*the night so cold*
*moonless  starry sky*
*and no sleep...*

*die Nacht ist so kalt*
*Sternenhimmel ohne Mond*
*und ohne Schlaf...*

*la nuit si froide.*
*ciel étoilé sans lune*
*et pas de sommeil...*

*la noche tan fría*
*cielo estrellado sin luna*
*y nada de sueño...*

279.

quanto tempo mais
o doce correr dos dias
nesta minha vida?

*how much longer*
*the sweet run of days*
*in this life of mine?*

*wie lange noch*
*der süße Lauf der Tage*
*in meinem Leben?*

*combien de temps encore*
*la douce course des jours*
*dans ma vie?*

*cuánto tiempo más*
*el dulce correr de los días*
*en esta mia vida?*

280.

como escolher –
o que nos eleva ou
o que dá prazer?

*how to choose –*
*what elevates us or*
*what gives pleasure?*

*wie zu wählen –*
*was erhebt uns oder*
*was macht Freude?*

*comment choisir –*
*ce qui nous élève ou*
*ce qui fait plaisir?*

*como elegir –*
*lo que nos eleva o*
*¿lo que nos place?*

281.

na vida é preciso
estar sempre alerta –
logo tudo muda!

*in life we need*
*to always be on alert –*
*soon everything changes!*

*im Leben muss man*
*immer wachsam sein –*
*bald ändert sich alles!*

*dans la vie il faut*
*toujours être en alerte –*
*bientôt tout change!*

*en la vida es necesario*
*estar siempre alerta –*
*¡muy pronto todo cambia!*

\*\*\*

282.

hoje vi o sol pôr
quando saí – dias mais longos
já meio inverno...

*today I saw the sun set*
*when I left – longer days*
*it's already midwinter...*

*heute sah ich den Sonnenuntergang*
*als ich ging – längere Tage*
*bereits mitten im Winter...*

*aujourd'hui j'ai vu le soleil se coucher*
*quand je suis sortie – des jours plus longs*
*déjà la mi-hiver...*

*hoy he visto la puesta del sol*
*cuando sali – días más largos*
*ya medio invierno...*

283.

morno dia de sol –
até os pássaros crêem
já ser primavera!

*warm sunny day –*
*even the birds believe*
*it´s spring already!*

*warmer sonniger Tag –*
*sogar die Vögel glauben*
*es sei schon Frühling!*

*chaude journée ensoleillée –*
*même les oiseaux croient*
*que c´est déjà le printemps!*

*día calido de sol –*
*hasta los pájaros creen*
*¡ya ser primavera!*

284.

numa árvore nua
esperando pela vida
um ninho vazio...

*on a bare tree*
*waiting for life*
*an empty nest...*

*auf einem kahlen Baum*
*warten auf das Leben*
*ein leeres Nest...*

*sur un arbre nu*
*en attendant la vie*
*un nid vide...*

*en un árbol desnudo*
*esperando la vida*
*un nido vacío...*

285.

as amendoeiras
já estão todas em flor –
tão brancas no verde

*the almond trees*
*are all in bloom –*
*so white on the green*

*die Mandelbäume*
*sind alle in voller Blüte –*
*so weiß in dem grün*

*les amandiers*
*sont tous en fleur –*
*si blancs sur le vert*

*los almendros*
*ya están todos en flor –*
*tan blancos en el verde*

\*\*\*

286.

quando se tem tudo
é fácil ser magnânimo –
e os que nada têm?...

*when one has everything*
*it is easy to be magnanimous –*
*and those who have nothing?...*

*wenn du alles hast*
*es ist leicht, großmütig zu sein –*
*und die, die nichts haben?...*

*quand on a tout*
*il est facile d'être magnanime –*
*et ceux qui n'ont rien?...*

*cuando se tiene todo*
*es fácil ser magnánimo –*
*y los que nada tienen?...*

287.

se eu já sabia
que vinha parar aqui
porque não fiz mais?...

*if I already knew*
*that was going to end here*
*why did not I do more?...*

*wenn ich schon wüsste*
*ich würde hier enden*
*warum habe ich nicht mehr getan?...*

*si je savais déjà*
*que j´allais finir ici*
*pourquoi n'ai-je pas fait plus?...*

*si yo ya sabía*
*que aquí llegaría*
*¿por qué no hice más?...*

\*\*\*

288.

cada dia que passa
mais incerto é o futuro –
como? até quando?...

*each day that passes by*
*the more uncertain is the future -*
*how? until when?...*

*jeder Tag, der vergeht*
*desto ungewisser ist die Zukunft -*
*wie? bis wann? ...*

*chaque jour qui passe*
*l'avenir est plus incertain -*
*comment? jusqu'à quand? ...*

*cada día que pasa*
*más incierto es el futuro -*
*¿cómo? ¿hasta cuando?...*

\*\*\*

289.

tão cedo ainda
nas árvores do jardim
já há rebentos!

*so early yet*
*in the trees of the garden*
*there are already shoots!*

*so früh noch*
*auf den Bäumen im Garten*
*es gibt bereits Sprossen!*

*si tôt encore*
*dans les arbres du jardin*
*il y a déjà des pousses!*

*tan pronto todavía*
*en los árboles del jardín*
*¡ya hay brotes!*

290.

lindas flores brancas
enfeitam a cameleira
ainda sem folhas

*beautiful white flowers*
*decorate the camellia tree*
*still without leaves*

*schöne weiße Blumen, die*
*den Kamelienbaum schmücken*
*noch ohne Blätter*

*belles fleurs blanches*
*décorent le camélia*
*encore sans feuilles*

*hermosas flores blancas*
*adornan la camelia*
*aún sin hojas*

\*\*\*

291.

pisei o deserto
só areia e estrelas
um outro mundo...

*I stepped on the desert*
*just sand and stars*
*another world...*

*ich betrat die Wüste*
*nur Sand und Sterne*
*eine andere Welt...*

*j'ai marché dans le désert*
*juste du sable et des étoiles*
*un autre monde...*

*pisé el desierto*
*solo arena y estrellas*
*otro mundo...*

292.

pedras erguidas
de encontro ao sol nascente
ecos dum passado...

*standing stones*
*against the rising sun*
*echoes of a past...*

*stehende Steine*
*gegen die aufgehende Sonne*
*Echos der Vergangenheit...*

*pierres dressées*
*contre le soleil levant*
*échos d'un passé...*

*piedras erigidas*
*contra el sol naciente*
*ecos de un pasado...*

\*\*\*

293.

dois longos anos
desta vida difícil –
mas estou viva!

*two long years*
*of this difficult life –*
*but I am alive!*

*zwei lange Jahre*
*von diesem schwierigen Leben –*
*aber ich bin noch am Leben!*

*deux longues années*
*de cette vie difficile –*
*mais je suis vivante!*

*dos largos años*
*de esta vida difícil –*
*pero estoy viva!*

294.

tudo tão bonito
flores de todas as cores –
mas é tão cedo!

*everything so beatiful*
*flowers of all colours –*
*but it´s so early!*

*alles so schön*
*Blumen in allen Farben –*
*aber es ist so früh!*

*tout est si beau*
*fleurs de toutes les couleurs –*
*mais c'est si tôt!*

*todo tan hermoso*
*flores de todos los colores –*
*pero es tan temprano!*

\*\*\*

295.

viver o momento
é o único segredo
da felicidade...

*to live in the moment
it's the only secret
of happiness...*

*leben im Moment
ist das einzige Geheimnis
des Glücks...*

*vivre dans le moment
c'est le seul secret
du bonheur....*

*vivir el momento
es el único secreto
de la felicidad...*

296.

hoje estou triste
talvez cansada – a vida
é tão complicada...

*today I feel sad
perhaps just tired – life
is so complicated...*

*heute bin ich traurig
vielleicht müde  –  das Leben
ist so kompliziert...*

*je suis triste aujourd'hui
peut-être fatiguée – la vie
est tellement compliquée...*

*hoy estoy triste
tal vez cansada – la vida
es tan difícil ...*

297.

dois anos passados –
o desejo de morrer
para descansar...

*two years have gone by –*
*the desire to die*
*to finally rest...*

*zwei Jahre später –*
*der Wunsch zu sterben*
*zur Ruhe...*

*deux ans plus tard –*
*le désir de mourir*
*pour me reposer...*

*dos años pasados –*
*el deseo de morir*
*para descansar...*

298.

tantos anos juntas
partilhando vidas
e muitas leituras

[dedicatória do meu livro de Haikus para as minhas amigas do grupo de leitura
– fevereiro de 2019]

*so many years together*
*sharing our lives*
*and so many books*

*so viele Jahre zusammen*
*Leben teilen*
*und viele Lesungen*

*tant d'années ensemble*
*à partager nos vies*
*et tant de lectures*

*tantos años juntas*
*compartiendo vidas*
*y muchas lecturas*

\*\*\*

299.

parece nevar…
mas são pétalas de flores
suspensas no vento

*it looks like it´s snowing…*
*but it´s only flower petals*
*suspended in the wind*

*es scheint zu schneien…*
*aber es sind Blütenblätter*
*im Wind aufgehängt*

*il semble neiger…*
*mais ce sont des pétales de fleurs*
*suspendues dans le vent*

*parece nevar…*
*pero son pétalos de flores*
*suspendidas en el viento*

300.

uns galhos no bico
no alto da árvore
o pássaro chama

*some branches in its beak*
*at the top of the tree*
*the bird calls*

*einige Äste im Schnabel*
*an der Spitze des Baumes*
*der Vogel ruft*

*quelques branches dans le bec*
*au sommet de l'arbre*
*l'oiseau appelle*

*una rama en el pico*
*en lo alto del árbol*
*el pájaro llama*

301.

manhã gloriosa –
em verde, cores e odores
vida a rebentar!

*glorious morning –*
*in green, colors and odors*
*life bursting!*

*herrlicher Morgen –*
*in grün, Farben und Düften*
*das Leben sprengt!*

*matin glorieux –*
*en vert, couleurs et odeurs*
*la vie éclatante!*

*mañana gloriosa –*
*en verde, colores y olores*
*¡vida estellando!*

302.

o som de asas
voando sob o céu tão azul –
instante de paz

*sound of wings*
*flying under the blue sky –*
*moment of peace*

*das Geräusch von Flügeln*
*fliegen unter einem blauen Himmel –*
*Augenblick des Friedens*

*son des ailes*
*volant sous le ciel si bleu –*
*moment de paix*

*sonido de las alas*
*volando bajo el cielo tan azul –*
*instante de paz*

\*\*\*

144

303.

sôfrega de água
depois da seca intensa –
andei à chuva...

*full of thirst*
*after the intense drought –*
*I walked in the rain...*

*Wasserfracht*
*nach intensiver Dürre –*
*ich bin im Regen gelaufen...*

*assoiffée d'eau*
*après la sécheresse intense –*
*j'ai marché sous la pluie...*

*ansiosa de agua*
*después de la sequía intensa –*
*caminé bajo la lluvia...*

304.

em fila indiana
pai, mãe e oito patinhos
passaram por mim

*in a row*
*father, mother and eight ducklings*
*passed me by*

*in einer Reihe*
*Vater, Mutter und acht Entenküken*
*gingen an mir vorbei*

*en file indienne*
*père, mère et huit canetons*
*sont passés devant moi*

*en fila india*
*padre, madre y ocho patitos*
*pasaron por mí*

305.

da minha janela
vejo um lindo mar azul –
sonho com viagens...

*from my window*
*I see a beautiful blue sea –*
*I dream of travels...*

*von meinem Fenster*
*sehe ich ein schönes blaues Meer –*
*ich träume von Reisen...*

*de ma fenêtre*
*je vois une belle mer bleue –*
*je rêve de voyages...*

*desde mi ventana*
*veo un hermoso mar azul –*
*sueño con viajes...*

306.

as andorinhas voam
em rápidos rodopios –
alegria de viver?

*the swallows fly*
*in quick turns –*
*joy of living?*

*die Schwalben fliegen*
*in schnellen Kurven –*
*Lebensfreude?*

*les hirondelles volent*
*en tourbillons rapides –*
*joie de vivre?*

*las golondrinas vuelan*
*en rápidos torbellinos –*
*alegría de vivir?*

307.

ninhos de cegonhas
cheios de novas vidas –
mundo renovado...

*stork nests*
*full of new lives –*
*world renewed...*

*Storchennester*
*vollvon neuem Leben –*
*erneuerte Welt...*

*nids de cigogne*
*plein de nouvelles vies –*
*monde renouvelé...*

*nidos de cigüeñas*
*llenos de nuevas vidas –*
*mundo renovado...*

308.

no meio do nada
um corvo passa a voar –
vida solitária...

*in the middle of nowhere*
*a crow flies –*
*solitary life...*

*Mitten im Nirgendwo*
*eine Krähe fliegt –*
*einsames Leben...*

*au milieu de nulle part*
*un corbeau s'envole –*
*vie solitaire...*

*en medio de la nada*
*un cuervo pasa volando –*
*vida solitaria...*

309.

lancei ao vento
papagaio de papel –
deixei-o fugir!

*I threw in the wind*
*a paper kyte –*
*I let it run away!*

*ich schlugden Papierdrachen*
*in den Wind –*
*ich habe ihn weglaufen lassen!*

*j'ai jeté au vent*
*un cerf-volant en papier –*
*je l´ai laissé fuir!*

*lancé al viento*
*cometa de papel –*
*le dejé huir!*

310.

por trás da árvore
o sol poente mergulha
num mar picado

*behind the tree*
*the setting sun dips*
*in a choppy sea*

*hinter dem Baum*
*die untergehende Sonne versinkt*
*in eine unruhigen See*

*derrière l'arbre*
*le soleil couchant plonge*
*dans une mer agitée*

*detrás del árbol*
*el sol poniente zambullido*
*en un mar revuelto*

311.

um céu amarelo
segue-se ao pôr do sol –
fim de mais um dia

*a yellow sky*
*follows the sunset –*
*end of another day*

*ein gelber Himmel*
*folgt dem Sonnenuntergang –*
*Ende eines weiteren Tages*

*un ciel jaune*
*suit le coucher du soleil –*
*fin d'une autre journée*

*un cielo amarillo*
*se sigue a la puesta del sol –*
*el fin de un día más*

312.

odor a maresia
o som das ondas do mar –
magnífica tarde!

*salty odor*
*the sound of ocean waves –*
*magnificent afternoon!*

*Geruch nash Salznebel*
*der Klang der Meereswellen –*
*herrlicher Nachmittag!*

*odeur salée*
*le son des vagues de l´océan –*
*magnifique après-midi!*

*olor a sal*
*el sonido de las olas del mar –*
*¡magnífica tarde!*

313.

verde é este rio
uma luz brilhante passa
e o vento o revolta

*green is this river*
*a bright light passes*
*and the wind revolves it*

*grün ist dieser Fluss*
*ein helles Licht zieht vorbei*
*und der Wind wirbelt es weg*

*vert est cette rivière*
*une lumière brillante passe*
*et le vent la retourne*

*verde es este río*
*una luz brillante pasa*
*y el viento lo levanta*

314.

fui sempre feliz
na casa da praia
meu pequeno limbo...

*I was always happy*
*at the beach house*
*my little limbo...*

*ich war immer glücklich*
*am Strandhaus*
*meine kleine Schwebe...*

*j'étais toujours heureuse*
*à la maison de plage*
*mon petit paradis...*

*siempre fui feliz*
*en la casa de la playa*
*mi pequeño limbo...*

315.
da minha janela
sinto o cheiro do mar
e o odor a seiva

*from my window*
*I smell the sea*
*and the odor of sap*

*von meinem Fenster*
*rieche ich das Meer*
*und der Saftgeruch*

*de ma fenêtre*
*je sens l'odeur de la mer*
*et l'odeur de la sève*

*desde mi ventana*
*siento el olor del mar*
*y de la savia*

316.
camadas de luz
laranja, rosa e anil –
fim de mais um dia

*layers of light*
*orange, pink and indigo –*
*end of another day*

*Schichten von Licht*
*orange, rosa und indigo –*
*Ende eines weiteren Tages*

*couches de lumière*
*orange, rose et indigo –*
*fin d'une autre journée*

*capas de luz*
*naranja, rosa e índigo –*
*fin de otro día*

317.

reflexos de água
verde intenso – arrozais
a perder de vista

water reflections
intense green – rice fields
reaching the horizon

Wasserreflexe
intensiv grün – Reisfelder
bis zum Horizont

reflets de l'eau
vert intense – rizières
jusqu'à l´horizon

reflejos de agua
verde intenso – arrozales
fuera de la vista

318.

no ar da manhã
um cheiro a terra molhada –
chuva de verão...

in the morning air
a smell of wet soil –
summer rain...

in der Morgenluft
ein Geruch von feuchtem Boden –
Sommerregen...

dans l'air du matin
une odeur de terre humide –
pluie d'été...

en el aire de la mañana
un olor a tierra mojada –
lluvia de verano...

319.

choveu de novo –
já não estalam as folhas
debaixo dos pés...

it rained again –
the leaves no longer crackle
under my feet...

es regnet wieder –
die Blätter knirschen nicht mehr
unter den Füßen...

il a encore plu –
les feuilles ne craquent plus
sous les pieds...

llovió de nuevo –
ya no rompen las hojas
bajo los pies...

320.

estranha é a vida:
tempos de muita beleza
e de tanta dor...

strange is this life:
times of great beauty
and so much pain...

seltsam ist das Leben:
Zeiten von großer Schönheit
und so viel Schmerz...

étrange est la vie:
des moments d'une grande beauté
et tellement de douleur...

extraña es la vida:
tiempos de gran belleza
y tanto dolor...

321.

asas vibrando –
borboleta da noite
de encontro à luz

*fluttering wings –*
*night butterfly*
*against the light*

*flatternde Flügel –*
*Nachtschmetterling*
*gegen das Licht*

*ailes battantes –*
*papillon de nuit*
*à contre-jour*

*aleteo de alas –*
*mariposa nocturna*
*contra la luz*

322.

na fria madrugada
só o som da borboleta
e do mar ao fundo

*in the cold dawn*
*only the sound of the butterfly*
*and the sea in the background*

*in der kalten Morgendämmerung*
*nur der Klang des Schmetterlings*
*und das Meer im Hintergrund*

*à l'aube froide*
*seul le son du papillon de nuit*
*et la mer en arrière plan*

*en el amanecer frio*
*solo el sonido de la mariposa*
*y del mar al fondo*

323.

madrugada clara
sem vento, o som do mar
e o tempo parado...

*clear dawn*
*no wind, the sound of the sea*
*and time stopped...*

*klare Morgendämmerung*
*kein Wind, das Rauschen des Meeres*
*und die Zeit blieb stehen...*

*aube claire*
*pas de vent, le bruit de la mer*
*et le temps arrêté...*

*amanecer claro*
*sin viento, el sonido del mar*
*y el tiempo detenido...*

324.

manhã já clara –
porque não se ouvem ainda
sons de passarinhos?

*already clear morning –*
*why don't I hear yet*
*bird sounds?*

*schon klarer Morgen –*
*warum hörst du noch nicht*
*Vogelstimmen?*

*le matin déjà clair –*
*pourquoi n'entends-je pas encore*
*les sons des oiseaux?*

*ya clara mañana –*
*por qué no escuchas todavía*
*sonidos de pájaros?*

325.

a musa da noite
voltou – não deu para dormir
mas gostei que viesse

*the muse of the night*
*came back – I couldn't sleep*
*but I liked it came*

*die Muse der Nacht*
*kam zurück – ich konnte nicht schlafen*
*aber ich mochte, dass sie kam*

*la muse de la nuit*
*est revenue – je n´ait pas dormi*
*mais j'ai aimé qu´elle vienne*

*la musa de la noche*
*regresó – no podía dormir*
*pero me alegró que viniera*

326.

a vida no mundo
flue em ritmos definidos
de que somos parte

*life in the world*
*flow at set rates*
*that we are part of*

*Leben in der Welt*
*fließt in bestimmten Rhythmen*
*von denen wir ein Teil sind*

*la vie dans le monde*
*coule dans des rythmes définis*
*dont nous faisons partie*

*la vida en este mundo*
*fluye en ritmos establecidos*
*de que hacemos parte*

327.
　　notei de repente
　　o irregular bater
　　do meu coração

　　　　　　　*I suddenly noticed*
　　　　　　　*the irregular beat*
　　　　　　　*of my heart*

　　　　　　　*ich bemerkte plötzlich*
　　　　　　　*das unregelmäßige Schlagen*
　　　　　　　*meines Herzens*

　　　　　　　*j'ai soudain remarqué*
　　　　　　　*le battement irrégulier*
　　　　　　　*de mon coeur*

　　　　　　　*de repente me di cuenta*
　　　　　　　*del golpe irregular*
　　　　　　　*de mi corazón*

　　　　　　　　*** 

328.
　　a suave neblina
　　o sol, o mar, o céu azul –
　　manhã gloriosa!

　　　　　　　*the soft fog*
　　　　　　　*the sun, the sea, the blue sky –*
　　　　　　　*glorious morning!*

　　　　*der weiche Nebel*
　　　　*die Sonne, das Meer, der blaue Himmel –*
　　　　*herrlicher Morgen!*

　　　　　　　*le doux brouillard*
　　　　　　　*le soleil, la mer, le ciel bleu –*
　　　　　　　*glorieux matin!*

　　　　　　　*la niebla suave*
　　　　　　　*el sol, el mar, el cielo azul –*
　　　　　　　*gloriosa mañana!*

329.

a neblina apaga
a linha do horizonte
para além do mar…

*the mist erases*
*the line of the horizin*
*beyond the sea…*

*der Nebel verschwindet*
*die Horizontlinie*
*jenseits des Meeres…*

*le brouillard éteint*
*la ligne de l´horizon*
*au-delà de la mer…*

*la niebla borra*
*la linea del horizonte*
*más allá del mar…*

330.

na tarde amena
a luz, a brisa, o silêncio –
refúgio do mundo…

*mild afternoon*
*the light, the breeze, the silence –*
*refuge from the world…*

*am milden Nachmittag*
*das Licht, die Brise, die Stille –*
*Zuflucht vor der Welt…*

*doux après-midi*
*la lumière, la brise, le silence –*
*refuge du monde…*

*en la tarde amena*
*la luz, la brisa, el silencio –*
*refugio del mundo…*

331.
há muito já mortos –
espíritos do passado
ruínas de vidas...

[escrito durante a visita às ruínas de Conimbriga, em setembro 2019]

*dead for so long –*
*spirits of the past*
*ruins of lives...*

*lange tot –*
*Geister der Vergangenheit*
*Ruinen des Lebens...*

*morts depuis longtemps –*
*esprits du passé*
*ruines de vies...*

*muertos hace mucho –*
*espíritus del pasado*
*ruinas de vidas ...*

332.
quase não há vento
o mar mal se ouve – terna
manhã de outono...

*almost no wind*
*the sea is barely heard – tender*
*autumn morning...*

*fast keinen Wind*
*Das Meer ist kaum zu hören – zart*
*Herbstmorgen...*

*presque pas de vent*
*la mer à peine audible – tendre*
*matin d'automne...*

*casi no hay viento*
*el mar apenas se oye – tierna*
*mañana de otoño...*

333.

num céu bem cinzento
as gaivotas voam livres
imunes ao frio...

*in a very gray sky*
*seagulls fly free*
*immune to the cold...*

*in einem sehr grauen Himmel*
*Möwen fliegen frei*
*immun gegen die Kälte...*

*dans un ciel très gris*
*les mouettes volent librement*
*insensibles au froid...*

*en un cielo muy gris*
*las gaviotas vuelan libres*
*inmunes al frío...*

334.

um pouco de água
e tudo brota de novo –
a força da vida!

*a little bit of water*
*and everything springs up again –*
*the force of life!*

*etwas Wasser*
*und alles springt wieder auf –*
*die Kraft des Lebens!*

*un peu d'eau*
*et tout recommence –*
*la force de la vie!*

*un poco de agua*
*y todo vuelve a brotar –*
*la fuerza de la vida!*

335.

manhã de outono.
no ar um forte odor
a mosto de azeitona

*autumn morning.*
*a strong odor in the air*
*of olive must*

*Herbstmorgen.*
*ein starker Geruch in der Luft*
*im Olivenmost*

*matin d'automne.*
*une forte odeur dans l'air*
*de moût d'olive*

*mañana de otoño.*
*un fuerte olor en el aire*
*a mosto de oliva*

336.

a santa rainha,
triste, contempla a planície
do alto da torre

[quando vamos ao Alentejo, lembro-me sempre da Rainha Santa Isabel, que
morreu na torre do Castelo de Estremoz, a tentar evitar que o marido e o filho
se confrontassem numa sangrenta batalha]

*the holy queen,*
*sad, watches the flat land*
*from the top of the tower*

*die heilige Königin,*
*traurig, erwägt die Ebene*
*von der Spitze des Turms*

*la sainte reine,*
*triste, regarde la plaine*
*du haut de la tour*

*la reina santa*
*triste, contempla la llanura*
*desde lo alto de la torre*

337.
no céu cinzento
espreita um raio de sol:
um arco-íris!

*in the gray sky*
*peeks a ray of sunshine:*
*a rainbow!*

*unter dem grauen Himmel*
*dort lauert ein Sonnenstrahl:*
*ein Regenbogen!*

*dans le ciel gris*
*le soleil jette un coup d'œil:*
*un arc-en-ciel!*

*en el cielo gris*
*asoma un rayo de sol:*
*un arcoiris!*

338.
frio, calor ou chuva
o autocarro acelera
às seis da manhã

*cold, heat or rain*
*the bus speeds up*
*at six in the morning*

*Kälte, Hitze oder Regen*
*der Bus wird schneller*
*um sechs Uhr morgens*

*froid, chaleur ou pluie*
*le bus accélère*
*à six heures du matin*

*frío, calor o lluvia*
*el autobús acelera*
*a las seis de la mañana*

339.
no jardim, bem cedo
volteiam velhos no ar
fazendo tai-chi

*in the garden, early*
*elders bounce in the air*
*practicing tai chi*

*im Garten, früh am Morgen*
*alte Männer drehen sich in der Luft*
*tai chi machen*

*dans le jardin, tôt*
*des vieux tournent dans l'air*
*pratiquant le tai-chi*

*en el jardín, temprano*
*viejos giran en el aire*
*haciendo tai-chi*

340.
zzzumbindo na noite
um só mosquito acorda
um desgraçado...

*buzzzzing in the night*
*only one mosquito wakes up*
*an unfortunate soul...*

*Summen in der Nacht*
*eine einzelne Mücke wacht auf*
*eine Unglückliche...*

*bourdonnement dans la nuit*
*un seul moustique réveille*
*un malheureux...*

*zumbando en la noche*
*un solo mosquito despierta*
*un desgraciado...*

341.

com um sobressalto
desperta o trabalhador
para mais um dia...

*with a little start*
*awakens the worker*
*for one more day...*

*mit einem Ruck*
*wacht den Arbeiter auf*
*für einen weiteren Tag...*

*avec un petit saut*
*se réveille le travailleur*
*pour un jour de plus...*

*con un pequeño sobresalto*
*despierta el trabajador*
*por un nuevo día...*

342.

na manhã gelada
enrolada como um feto
debaixo da roupa

*in the cold morning*
*rolled up like a fetus*
*under the blankets*

*am eiskalten Morgen*
*zusammengerollt wie ein Fötus*
*unter der Kleidung*

*dans le matin froid*
*enroulée comme un fœtus*
*sous les couvertures*

*en la mañana helada*
*enroscada como un feto*
*debajo de la ropa*

343.
as manhãs de sol,
um frio cortante na cara –
já cheira a natal!

*sunny mornings,*
*a sharp cold in the face –*
*already smells like christmas!*

*sonnige Morgen,*
*eine scharfe Erkältung im Gesicht –*
*es riecht schon nach Weihnachten!*

*matins ensoleillés,*
*un froid tranchant le visage –*
*ça sent déjà noël!*

*mañanas soleadas,*
*frío punzante en la cara –*
*¡ya huele a navidad!*

344.
tapetes de folhas
cobrem as ruas da cidade –
inverno a chegar...

*leaf mats*
*cover the city streets –*
*winter is coming...*

*Blattmatten*
*bedecke die Straßen der Stadt –*
*der Winter kommt...*

*des tapis de feuilles*
*couvrent les rues de la ville –*
*l'hiver arrive...*

*alfombras de hojas*
*cubren las calles de la ciudad –*
*el invierno llegando...*

345.

uma chuva forte
molha as terras ressequidas –
sede mitigada...

*a heavy rain*
*wets the parched lands –*
*mitigated thirst...*

*ein starker Regen*
*benetzt das ausgedörrten Länder –*
*gemilderter Durst...*

*une forte pluie*
*mouille les terres desséchées –*
*soif atténuée...*

*una fuerte lluvia*
*moja las tierras resecas –*
*sed mitigada...*

346.

as ruas molhadas
da chuva toda que caiu
e um ar mais limpo

*the wet streets*
*of all the rain that fell*
*and a cleaner air*

*die nassen Straßen*
*von all dem Regen, der fiel*
*und eine saubere Luft*

*les rues mouillées*
*de toute la pluie qui est tombée*
*et un air plus pur*

*las calles mojadas*
*de toda la lluvia que cayó*
*y el aire más limpio*

347.
nuvens de asas pretas
rufando no céu azul –
são as andorinhas!

[uma primavera, na Galé, assisti à chegada das andorinhas, em nuvens negras
de milhares de pássaros negros voando para norte]

*clouds of black wings*
*drumming in the blue sky –*
*it's the swallows!*

*schwarz geflügelte Wolken*
*Rascheln im blauen Himmel –*
*es sind die Schwalben!*

*nuages d'ailes noires*
*battant dans le ciel bleu –*
*ce sont les hirondelles!*

*nubes de alas negras*
*tamborileando en el cielo azul –*
*son las golondrinas!*

348.
o velho melro
já nem levanta vôo
quando alguém passa

*the old blackbird*
*no longer takes flight*
*when someone passes*

*die alte Amsel*
*fliegt nicht mehr*
*wenn jemand geht*

*le vieux merle*
*ne prend plus son envol*
*quand quelqu'un passe*

*el viejo mirlo*
*ya ni levanta vuelo*
*cuando alguien pasa*

349.

um rufar de asas
passou por cima de mim –
olhei e nada vi...

*a roll of wings*
*passed over my head –*
*I looked and saw nothing...*

*ein Flügelschlag*
*flog über mich hinweg –*
*ich schaute und sah nichts...*

*un battement d'ailes*
*est passé au dessus de moi –*
*j'ai regardé et je n'ai rien vu...*

*un aleteo*
*pasó sobre mí cabeza –*
*miré y no vi nada...*

350.

lenha a crepitar
cheiro a torradas e chá –
odores de inverno...

*crackling firewood*
*smell of toast and tea –*
*winter scents...*

*Holzknistern*
*Geruch von Toast und Tee –*
*Der Winter riecht...*

*bois crépitant*
*odeur de pain grillé et de thé –*
*parfums d'hiver...*

*crepitar de leña*
*olor a té y tostadas –*
*olores de invierno...*

351.

um vento frio sopra
a chuva cai sem parar –
mas é tempo dela...

*a cold wind blows*
*the rain falls non-stop –*
*but it's its season...*

*ein kalter Wind weht*
*der Regen fällt ohne Unterbrechung –*
*aber es ist ihre Zeit...*

*un vent froid souffle*
*la pluie tombe sans arrêt –*
*mais c'est leur saison...*

*sopla un viento frío*
*la lluvia cae sin parar –*
*pero es su tiempo...*

352.

já estão a morrer
as flores do meu jasmim –
o odor ainda no ar...

*already dying*
*the flowers of my jasmine –*
*the odor still in the air...*

*sterben bereits*
*die Blumen meines Jasmins –*
*der Geruch noch in der Luft...*

*déjà en train de mourir*
*les fleurs de mon jasmin –*
*l'odeur toujours dans l'air...*

*ya están muriendo*
*las flores de mi jazmín –*
*su aroma aún en el aire...*

353.

a partir de hoje
oficialmente velha –
e chove lá fora…

[no meu 65º aniversário]

*as of today*
*officially an old woman –*
*and it rains outside...*

*ab heute*
*offiziell eine alte Frau –*
*und es regnet draußen...*

*à partir d'aujourd'hui*
*officiellement vieille –*
*et il pleut dehors...*

*a partir de hoy*
*oficialmente vieja –*
*y llueve afuera...*

354.

tão súbita e grave
esta mudança no mundo –
sobreviverei?

[sobre a pandemia de Covid-19, que surgiu na China em dezembro de 2019 e que rapidamente se espalhou pelo mundo inteiro, e que pela alta contagiosidade e elevada mortlidade, sobretudo em idosos e grupos de risco, obrigou todos os governos a tomar medidas extremas de isolamento e consequente descalabro económico e social].

*so sudden and serious*
*this change in the world –*
*will I survive?*

*so plötzlich und ernst*
*diese Veränderung in der Welt –*
*werde ich überleben?*

*si soudain et sérieux*
*ce changement dans le monde –*
*vais-je survivre?*

*tan repentino y serio*
*este cambio en el mundo –*
*sobreviviré?*

355.

o dia já nasceu
os passarinhos já cantam –
tudo recomeça...

*the day is already born*
*the birds are already singing –*
*everything starts over...*

*der Tag ist bereits geboren*
*die vögel singen schon –*
*alles fängt von vorne an...*

*le jour est déjà né*
*les oiseaux chantent déjà –*
*tout recommence...*

*el dia ya ha nacido*
*los pájaros cantando –*
*todo comienza de nuevo...*

356.

um novo dia bem –
terei um anjo da guarda
a velar por mim?...

*a new day still well –*
*do I have a guardian angel*
*watching over me?...*

*ein neuer guter Tag –*
*Ich werde einen Schutzengel haben*
*der über mich wacht?...*

*un jour de plus, je vais bien –*
*aurai-je un ange gardien*
*veillant sur moi?...*

*un día más estoy bien –*
*tendré un ángel guardián*
*¿velando-me?...*

357.
a velha águia plana
na escaldante brisa da tarde
de mais um verão

*the old eagle glides*
*in the hot afternoon breeze*
*of another summer*

*der alte Adler plättet*
*in der heißen Nachmittagsbrise*
*eines weiteren Sommers*

*le vieil aigle glisse*
*dans la brise chaude de l'après-midi*
*d´un nouvel été*

*la vieja águila desliza*
*en la cálida brisa de la tarde*
*de otro verano*

358.
do alto da torre
a triste rainha contempla
passado e futuro...

*from the top of the tower*
*the sad queen contemplates*
*past and future...*

*von der Spitze des Turms*
*die traurige Königin sinnt nach*
*Vergangenheit und Zukunft...*

*du haut de la tour*
*la reine triste contemple*
*passé et futur...*

*desde lo alto de la torre*
*la reina triste contempla*
*pasado y futuro...*

359.

vejo a velha torre
e quase consigo sentir
a dor da rainha...

*I see the old tower*
*and I can almost feel*
*the queen's pain...*

*ich sehe den alten Turm*
*und ich kann fast fühlen*
*der Schmerz der Königin...*

*je vois la vieille tour*
*et je peux presque sentir*
*la douleur de la reine...*

*veo la vieja torre*
*y casi puedo sentir*
*el dolor de la reina...*

360.

ouço mas não vejo
uma gaivota que pia
no céu de verão

*I hear but I can't see*
*a seagull that chirps*
*in the summer sky*

*ich höre, aber ich sehe nicht*
*eine Möwe, die zwitschert*
*unter dem Sommerhimmel*

*j'entends mais je ne vois pas*
*une mouette qui ricane*
*dans le ciel d'été*

*escucho pero no veo*
*una gaviota que canta*
*en el cielo de verano*

173

361.

dias curtos, chuva,
frio – e tanto tempo até
vir a primavera!

*short days, rain,*
*cold – and so long until*
*the spring comes!*

*kurze Tage, Regen,*
*kalt – und so lange bis der*
*der Frühling kommt!*

*jours courts, pluie,*
*froid – et si longtemps jusqu'à*
*ce que vienne le printemps!*

*días cortos, lluvia,*
*frío – y tanto tiempo hasta*
*que llegue la primavera*

362.

a chuva cai forte –
ouço correr nas caleiras
água preciosa

*the rain falls hard –*
*I hear running in the gutters*
*precious water*

*der Regen fällt stark –*
*ich höre auf den Dachrinnen*
*kostbares Wasser rennen*

*la pluie tombe fort –*
*j'entends courir sur les gouttières*
*eau précieuse*

*la lluvia cae fuerte –*
*la oigo correr por las alcantarillas*
*preciosa agua*

363.

a álveola-alba
saltita pelo passeio
abanando a cauda

*the white wagtail*
*skips on the sidewalk*
*wagging the tail*

*die Bachstelze*
*springt auf der Promenade*
*mit dem wedelden Schwanz*

*la bergeronnette printanière*
*saute sur le trottoir*
*en remuant la queue*

*la aguzanieves*
*salta en la caminata*
*meneando la cola*

364.

cinco da manhã.
no silêncio o som dum carro –
mais um novo dia

*five in the morning.*
*in the silence the sound of a car –*
*another new day*

*fünf Uhr morgens.*
*in der Stille das Geräusch eines Autos –*
*ein weiterer neuer Tag*

*cinq heures du matin.*
*dans le silence le bruit d'une voiture –*
*un nouveau jour de plus*

*cinco de la mañana.*
*en el silencio el sonido de un coche –*
*otro nuevo dia*

365.

semana no fim –
esperança dum descanso
que logo acaba...

*week at the end –*
*hope for a rest*
*which soon ends...*

*Woche am Ende –*
*Hoffnung auf Erholung*
*die bald vorbei sein wird...*

*en fin de semaine –*
*espoir d´un repos*
*qui se termine bientôt...*

*final de semana –*
*esperanza de un descanso*
*que pronto termina...*

366.

numa manhã fria
um rabirruivo esvoaça
na árvore nua

*on a cold morning*
*a roaring roarer flies*
*in the bare tree*

*an einem kalten Morgen*
*ein Quaste flattert*
*unter dem kahlen Baum*

*un matin froid*
*un rougequeue vole*
*dans l'arbre nu*

*en una mañana fría*
*un pájaro de cola roja revolotea*
*en el árbol desnudo*

176

www.ingramcontent.com/pod-product-compliance
Lightning Source LLC
Chambersburg PA
CBHW071353120626
46546CB00002B/675